Love That Lasts

A Clear Guide to Communication Skills for Couples Who Want Deeper Connection

Taylor Kade

Contents

prologue ... 1

Part 1
The Foundation of Safe Communication

1. Emotional Safety: The Ground for Real Connection ... 7
2. Listening That Makes Your Partner Feel Understood ... 18
3. Speaking Your Needs Clearly and Kindly ... 31

Part 2
Understanding Patterns and Emotional Triggers

4. Why You React the Way You Do ... 51
5. The Three Connection Styles ... 66
6. Turning Conflict Into Collaboration ... 81

Part 3
Conversations That Build Closeness

7. Daily Connection Habits ... 99
8. Deeper Conversations About Meaning and Identity ... 116
9. Intimacy and Desire Differences ... 130

Part 4
The Hard Talks Every Couple Eventually Faces

10. Money: One of the Biggest Communication Stressors ... 149
11. Trust, Mistakes and Repairing After Hurt ... 166
12. Technology, Distraction and Presence ... 184

Part 5
Staying Connected for the Long Run

13. Creating a Shared Future	203
14. When You Need Outside Help	219

Part 6
Workbook Appendix

Emotional Safety and Communication Foundations	237
Understanding Patterns and Triggers	241
Conflict and Repair Skills	243
Daily and Deep Connection Practices	245
Intimacy and Trust Healing Tools	249
Technology, Presence and Balance	253
Future Planning and Long Term Connection	255
Seven Day Connection Reset Worksheets	257
The 30 Day Connection Journey	271

prologue

Most couples want the same things. They want to feel close. They want to feel like a team. They want to feel understood and supported.

Yet even couples who care deeply about each other struggle to communicate about the simplest things. A question meant with kindness gets taken the wrong way. A small request turns into an argument. A moment when someone needs comfort becomes a moment when both people feel alone. None of this means the relationship is broken. It simply means the conversation habits that hold a relationship together need attention.

Healthy love is built in ordinary moments. It grows in how two people speak to each other when they are tired, busy or unsure. It deepens when they can talk openly about what hurts and what helps. It strengthens each time they understand each other a little more clearly. Communication is not only a skill. It is the daily path toward connection.

In real life, most problems begin long before the argument appears. They begin when partners avoid difficult topics, guess instead of asking, or hide needs because they worry about sounding demanding. They begin when stress and old experiences shape reactions without anyone realizing it. They begin when one person tries to talk and the other feels overwhelmed or misunderstood. These moments accumulate and slowly create distance. The good news is that the solution is simple and learnable. The way couples speak to each other can change everything.

> This book is designed to help you build a communication style that creates closeness instead of conflict.

You will learn how to talk in ways that make your partner feel safe, valued and understood. You will learn how to express needs without criticism, how to listen without getting defensive and how to slow down difficult conversations before they turn into arguments. You will discover your emotional patterns and learn how to respond gently to your partner's patterns. You will gain the tools to handle tough topics like money, intimacy, trust and technology without drifting apart.

Every chapter gives you clear examples and short scripts. You will see how the same conversation can happen in two ways. One path creates tension. The other path creates connection. You will also find simple exercises that help you apply the ideas to your own relationship. These are designed to take only a few minutes but can create meaningful change in how you talk and how you understand each other.

You do not need to communicate perfectly to have a loving relationship. You only need habits that make room for honesty, curiosity and care. When both partners feel emotionally safe, they become more generous. They listen more easily. They soften more quickly. They repair misunderstandings before they turn into deeper wounds. Communication becomes a bridge rather than a barrier.

> Love that lasts is not built on luck. It is built on two people choosing connection over winning, kindness over defensiveness and clarity over guessing.

The skills in this book give you practical ways to do that. Whether you are building a new relationship or strengthening one that has lasted for years, these tools will help you create the closeness you want.

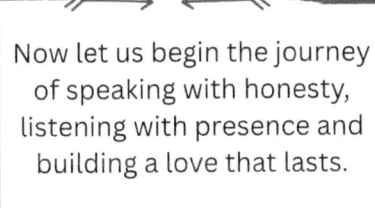

Now let us begin the journey of speaking with honesty, listening with presence and building a love that lasts.

Part 1
The Foundation of Safe Communication

Chapter 1
Emotional Safety: The Ground for Real Connection

Every strong relationship is built on one essential feeling. It is the sense that you can speak openly without being attacked or dismissed. It is the sense that your emotions matter to the other person. It is the sense that you will not be punished for telling the truth. This is emotional safety. Without it, couples avoid honest conversations, protect themselves instead of opening up and react instead of listening. With it, they can work through almost anything.

Many couples believe they have communication problems when the deeper issue is that they do not feel safe enough to be vulnerable. When safety is missing, a simple question can sound like criticism. A small irritation can feel like rejection. A request for help can feel like a demand. Emotions rise quickly because both partners feel unprotected. They act out of defense instead of connection.

Emotional safety does not mean avoiding difficult conversations. It means creating a space where both people can talk about anything without fear of being judged or rejected. It means knowing that your partner is on your side even when you disagree. It means trusting that both of you want to understand each other rather than win. When that trust is present, communication becomes easier and more honest. When it is absent, even the smallest interactions can turn tense.

Before learning how to speak your needs or listen with presence, you

must understand how safety works in relationships. Once you see the patterns that threaten it and the habits that protect it, your communication will shift in powerful ways.

What Emotional Safety Really Is

Emotional safety is the experience of being able to share your inner world without fear. It is not only about comfort. It is about trust. When you feel safe with someone, you believe they will not punish your vulnerability. You believe they will try to understand your feelings instead of attacking your character. You believe they want to make the relationship stronger, not score points.

Safety is created through tone, pacing, curiosity and consistency. It grows when partners show patience, ask questions and acknowledge each other's feelings. It grows when both people choose calm conversation over reactive behavior. It grows when mistakes are treated as learning moments rather than opportunities to shame or blame.

Humans are wired for emotional safety. Our nervous systems scan for signs of threat even in peaceful moments. A quick sigh, a raised eyebrow, a sharp tone or a long silence can trigger old fears and create distance. This is why couples need communication habits that bring both people back to calm connection.

When safety is present, couples can talk about disappointments, misunderstandings and hopes for change. They can share needs honestly. They can hear feedback without feeling attacked. Safety creates room for growth. It creates room for closeness. It creates room for deeper love.

Why Everything Depends on Safety

Many couples try to fix communication by changing the words they use. Words matter, but safety matters more. Without safety, even the perfect sentence can land badly. With safety, imperfect words can still bring partners closer.

Here is why safety comes first:

Safety keeps reactions low.

When you trust your partner's intention, you stay calmer during difficult conversations. Calm minds listen better. Calm hearts speak more honestly.

Safety encourages vulnerability.

When partners feel safe, they share fears, dreams and needs. These deeper truths build intimacy.

Safety reduces defensiveness.

If you believe your partner cares, you do not need to protect yourself through arguments or withdrawal.

Safety increases patience.

You give each other more grace when you believe the relationship is solid.

Safety turns conflict into teamwork.

> Disagreements become shared problems, not battles.

Without safety, couples lean into self protection. With safety, they lean into connection. This chapter teaches you how to build that foundation so everything else in this book can work for you.

The Four Biggest Safety Breakers

Most threats to emotional safety fall into four patterns. These patterns show up in almost every struggling relationship. Recognizing them is the first step toward changing them.

1. Criticism

Criticism sounds like blame and judgment. It points out flaws in character instead of addressing specific behaviors. It is often delivered with frustration or disappointment. Even mild criticism can feel like an attack.

Examples: "You never listen to me." "You are so selfish." "Why do you always have to ruin everything?" "I cannot rely on you for anything."

Criticism destroys safety because it suggests that something is wrong with your partner as a person. People defend themselves when they feel judged. They shut down, argue or attack back.

Replace criticism with clarity about your feelings and needs. Focus on the situation rather than the character of your partner.

2. Contempt

Contempt is the most damaging safety breaker. It includes insults, sarcasm, name calling and eye rolling. It carries an unspoken message: I am better than you. I am disgusted with you. I do not respect you.

Examples: "Seriously. That is the best you can do?" "You are ridiculous." "What a joke." "I cannot believe I am stuck with this."

Contempt destroys trust more quickly than any other behavior. It makes partners feel small and unvalued. Couples that rely on contempt create deep emotional wounds that are difficult to repair.

Respect must be protected at all times. If contempt shows up often, slow down and explore the feelings underneath it. Contempt usually hides hurt, insecurity or exhaustion.

3. Defensiveness

Defensiveness is natural, but it blocks understanding. It happens when your partner shares a concern and you respond by protecting your ego instead of listening.

Examples: "I did not do that." "You are exaggerating." "You are the one who always does that." "Why are you attacking me?"

Defensiveness sends the message that your partner's experience is wrong or irrelevant. It shuts down the possibility of connection.

The solution is to pause, breathe and hear the emotion behind your partner's words. You do not need to agree in order to be understanding. You only need to show that you care.

4. Withdrawal

Withdrawal happens when someone shuts down or disconnects. It can look like silence, walking away, avoiding eye contact or staying busy to escape the conversation. It can also look like being physically present but emotionally absent.

Examples: "Responding only with short answers." "Leaving the room without saying anything." "Staring at a phone instead of participating." "Saying it is fine when it is not."

Withdrawal is often self protection, not punishment. Yet it creates distance and confusion. The other partner feels abandoned or ignored.

Instead of withdrawing, ask for a short pause. Say that you need time to calm down and will come back. This creates safety rather than uncertainty.

· · ·

How to Create a Safe Atmosphere for Talking

Emotional safety is built through small, thoughtful habits. You do not need perfect communication skills to create safety. You only need consistent kindness and clear signals of care.

Here are the most effective ways to build safety during conversations.

1. Speak with a calm tone

Tone carries far more meaning than words. A gentle voice helps your partner stay calm. A harsh tone signals danger. Speak slowly and softly, especially when talking about hard topics.

2. Stay curious

Ask questions that show interest. Curiosity lowers defensiveness and invites openness.

Try questions like: Can you help me understand what felt hard?

What was going on inside you in that moment?

What do you need from me right now?

Curiosity is a sign of emotional safety.

3. Acknowledge feelings

Validation does not mean agreement. It means recognizing your partner's experience as real and important.

Examples:

I can see why that hurt.

That makes sense.

Thank you for telling me.

Validation softens tension and encourages trust.

4. Slow the conversation down

Fast conversations often lead to misunderstandings. Slowing the pace gives both people room to think and respond thoughtfully.

Use phrases like:

Let us take a moment.

I want to understand you better.

I hear you, and I am thinking about what you said.

5. Share your internal world

Safety grows when partners share what they feel, not only what they think.

Instead of saying: You never help.

Say: I felt overwhelmed today and needed support.

Sharing your inner experience makes it easier for your partner to connect with you instead of defending themselves.

6. Take breaks when needed

Breaks are not abandonment. They are emotional resets. A short pause can prevent the spiral that leads to hurtful behavior. Breaks work best when both people know exactly when the conversation will continue.

7. Show appreciation often

Small expressions of gratitude create a climate of warmth. Appreciation reminds both partners that they are valued even when there are conflicts to solve.

Exercise: Your Personal Triggers and Calming Plan

This exercise helps you understand what threatens your sense of safety and what helps restore it.

Step 1: Identify your triggers

Write down three moments that often make you feel defensive or overwhelmed. Examples include tone of voice, being interrupted, raised volume or certain topics.

Step 2: Identify the deeper emotion

For each trigger, ask yourself: What feeling does this bring up. Hurt. Fear. Shame. Anger. Exhaustion.

Step 3: Create a calming plan

List three actions that help you return to calm. Examples include breathing slowly, asking for a pause, stepping outside for fresh air or placing a hand on your chest to ground yourself.

Step 4: Share your plan with your partner

Tell your partner what helps you stay calm and what pulls you into stress. Invite them to share their own triggers and calming tools. These conversations build trust and empathy.

SCRIPTS FOR SAVE COMMUNICATION

These simple phrases help set a tone of care and connection.

Script for starting a gentle conversation

I want to talk about something but I want us both to feel safe. Can we take a moment and slow this down.

Script for taking space without creating distance

I am starting to feel overwhelmed. I need a short break so I can come back and listen better.

Use these phrases often. They protect the relationship during emotional moments and help both partners return to connection.

Emotional safety is the soil where communication grows. Without it, partners protect themselves instead of opening up. With it, they relax, listen, share and repair. Safety transforms ordinary conversations into moments of connection. It turns the relationship into a place where both partners can bring their full selves without fear.

You are not aiming for perfection. You are aiming for habits that create comfort, honesty and care. If you build safety first, every other skill in this book becomes easier. You will understand each other more clearly, argue less often and recover from misunderstandings more quickly. Safety gives love a steady home.

When partners feel safe, they grow together. When they feel unsafe, they grow apart. Your goal is to work as a team, not opponents. Safety makes that possible.

In the next chapter, we explore how to listen in a way that makes your partner feel understood at a deep level. True listening is one of the strongest sources of emotional safety. You will learn how to listen with presence, patience and curiosity so that your partner feels fully seen and valued.

Chapter 2
Listening That Makes Your Partner Feel Understood

Most people believe they are good listeners. They nod, wait for their turn and follow the general idea of what the other person is saying. Yet when couples describe their struggles, one theme appears again and again. One partner feels unheard, misunderstood or dismissed. The speaker believes they are communicating clearly, and the listener believes they are paying attention, yet somehow both walk away feeling disconnected. This is because real listening requires much more than being physically present. It requires emotional presence, curiosity and a willingness to understand before responding.

> Listening is the most powerful tool for building connection.

When your partner feels understood, they feel valued. They relax. They soften. They open up. They trust you with more of their inner world. Understanding creates closeness even when you disagree. Lack of understanding creates distance even when you want to feel close.

This chapter focuses on how to listen in a way that strengthens emotional safety, deepens connection and reduces conflict. The skills may feel simple, but they are transformative. Most relationship breakthroughs begin not with clever communication strategies, but with one person listening with patience, presence and genuine interest.

Why Most People Listen to Reply Instead of Listening to Understand

Human beings are wired to respond quickly. When someone speaks, our minds immediately start creating interpretations, analysis and counterpoints. We prepare responses before the other person finishes their sentence. We compare what they say with our own experiences. We focus on the parts that affect us personally. We become judges and problem solvers instead of listeners.

This habit is automatic. It comes from survival instincts. In stressful situations, the brain scans for threat and prepares a defense. Even in calm conversations, the mind often tries to protect the ego by planning what to say next. This is why listening requires conscious effort. Without that effort, we fall into patterns that block understanding.

Here are the most common reasons people listen to reply instead of listening to understand.

Fear of being wrong or blamed

When a partner shares a concern, the listener may hear an accusation or criticism, even when none was intended. This triggers a need to defend. Defensiveness shifts the mind away from understanding and toward self protection.

Desire to fix the problem

Many people believe that love means offering solutions. They listen only long enough to identify a problem and then switch into problem solving mode. The intention is positive, but the effect is that the speaker feels unseen. They were looking for empathy, not instructions.

Emotional overload

Strong feelings can make it difficult to hear someone else clearly. When a topic touches your own fears, insecurities or frustrations, your mind becomes busy. You focus on your own emotions rather than your partner's words.

Habitual interruption

Some people grow up in environments where interruptions are normal. They jump in with thoughts, reactions or stories. They believe they are participating, but the speaker feels cut off.

Assumptions and mind reading

It is easy to believe you already know what your partner is going to say. This leads to tuning out or responding based on assumptions rather than actual listening.

Distraction

Phones, screens and multitasking make true listening almost impossible. Even small distractions make the speaker feel secondary.

Understanding these obstacles is the first step. The second step is learning habits that quiet the mind and help you focus on your partner's experience.

Presence: The Foundation of Real Listening

Presence means giving your full attention without drifting mentally or emotionally. It means being in the moment instead of preparing your next thought. Presence makes your partner feel valued and respected. It also helps you understand the deeper meaning behind their words.

Here are the essential elements of presence.

Physical presence

Face your partner. Put down anything in your hands. Reduce background noise. Sit or stand in a position that shows availability. You do not need to stare intensely, but gentle eye contact helps your partner feel seen.

Mental presence

Set aside your internal commentary. You will notice thoughts rising up. That is normal. Acknowledge them and gently return to listening. Remind yourself that your goal is not to respond. Your goal is to understand.

Emotional presence

Stay curious about your partner's feelings. Try to sense the emotion under their words. Are they sad. Frustrated. Tired. Anxious. Lonely. Your presence becomes stronger when you attune to these emotional

Nonverbal signals

Your body language communicates more than your words. Lean slightly forward. Keep your arms relaxed. Nod occasionally. Show warmth in your face. These small signals reassure your partner that they matter.

Presence takes practice because it requires slowing down. Yet the benefits are profound. When you are truly present, your partner feels safe enough to express vulnerable emotions. They feel valued enough to open up more deeply. Presence alone can defuse tension and build closeness.

Curiosity: The Heart of Understanding

Curiosity is the willingness to explore your partner's inner world without judgment. It invites deeper sharing and reveals hidden layers of meaning. When you approach conversations with curiosity, your partner feels respected and cared for.

Curiosity asks gentle questions such as:

What made that moment hard for you?

What were you hoping for?

What did you need right then?

What part of this felt most important?

What does this situation remind you of?

Curiosity slows down conversations and turns them into discovery. Many conflicts disappear when one partner becomes genuinely curious about the other's feelings. Curiosity transforms arguments into learning moments. It shows your partner that you care more about understanding them than being right.

Here are the keys to healthy curiosity:

Ask open questions

Open questions invite deeper answers. Closed questions shut down conversation.

Closed question: Are you upset.

Open question: What is going on inside you right now.

Closed question: Did you mean to hurt me.

Open question: What were you feeling when that happened.

Avoid interrogation

Curiosity feels warm and slow. Interrogation feels sharp and demanding. Keep your tone soft and your pacing calm.

Stay neutral

Do not assume you know the answer to your question. Curiosity works only when you are genuinely open to whatever your partner says.

Let silence work for you

Sometimes your partner needs a quiet moment to think. Silence invites deeper reflection. Resist the urge to fill it.

Curiosity brings understanding. Understanding brings closeness.

. . .

Reflective Listening: The Skill That Makes People Feel Safe

Reflective listening is the most powerful listening technique couples can use. It involves restating or summarizing what your partner said in your own words. This shows that you heard them and that you are trying to understand what they mean.

Some people worry that reflective listening sounds unnatural, but when done with warmth, it feels deeply supportive. It slows down the conversation and helps both partners understand each other more clearly.

Here is how reflective listening works:

Listen fully before responding

Let your partner finish their thought. Do not interrupt or jump in.

Reflect the content

Repeat the main idea in your own words.

Example:

You are feeling stressed because you felt alone with the chores today. Did I understand that correctly.

Reflect the emotion

Identify the emotion behind their words.

Example:

It sounds like you felt unappreciated and overwhelmed.

Confirm your understanding

Ask if you got it right.

Example:

Did I hear that accurately.

or

What I hear you saying is that you needed support and felt let down. Did I get that right.

Adjust if needed

If your partner says you missed something, reflect again. This is not failure. It is deepening the connection.

Reflective listening is not about repeating words mechanically. It is about giving your partner the experience of being fully understood. That experience alone softens tension, builds trust and creates emotional intimacy.

How to Respond Without Fixing or Debating

Many conversations fall apart because the listener jumps into problem solving or defending. When your partner shares feelings, they are not asking you to fix the situation or argue your point. They want to feel understood. Understanding must come before any solutions or explanations.

Here are the steps for responding without fixing or debating.

Validate their emotion

Validation is acknowledgment. It does not mean agreement.

Examples:

I hear how upsetting that was for you.

That makes sense.

Thank you for telling me.

Validation reassures your partner that their feelings matter.

Avoid explanations until after understanding

Even a gentle explanation can sound defensive if offered too soon.

Instead of saying: I did not mean it that way.

Try: I can see how that affected you. I want to understand you fully before I explain my side.

Resist the urge to solve

Your partner might need comfort more than solutions.

Instead of: Next time just tell me earlier.

Try: I am here with you. Tell me more about how that felt.

Solutions can come later. Emotional connection must come first.

Keep the focus on their experience

Reflect what they are saying.

What mattered most in that moment for you.

It sounds like that left you feeling alone.

Center their experience before bringing in your own.

Share your perspective gently and only when the moment is right

Once your partner feels understood, they will be more open to your thoughts. At this point you can share your feelings or insights without causing defensiveness.

Example:

Now that I understand you better, I want to share what happened on my side so we can work through this together.

Responding without fixing or debating takes patience. Yet it leads to less conflict and more connection.

The Power of Feeling Understood

When someone feels understood, the whole emotional atmosphere changes. Their body relaxes. Their tone softens. Their frustration eases. Their defenses lower. They feel cared for. They feel valued. They feel connected.

Feeling understood is one of the most intimate experiences in a relationship. It creates trust. It builds emotional safety. It strengthens the bond between partners. Many couples discover that most of their arguments fade once both people feel heard.

Listening well also changes the listener. It helps you become more compassionate, more patient and more attuned to your partner. These qualities enrich the entire relationship.

Exercise: Five Minute Mirror and Repeat Practice

This exercise strengthens presence, curiosity and reflective listening. It also reveals how much meaning gets lost when couples assume they understand each other.

Do this exercise at a calm moment. Set a timer for five minutes.

Step 1: Partner A speaks

Partner A talks for one minute about something simple but meaningful. It can be a recent event, a memory or a thought. No interruptions are allowed.

Step 2: Partner B mirrors

Partner B repeats back the main idea and the emotion they heard. Use gentle phrasing such as:

What I hear you saying is that you felt grateful for the support from your friend. Did I get that right.

or

It sounds like you were frustrated because your day felt chaotic. Did I understand correctly.

Partner B checks for accuracy. Partner A corrects anything that is off and adds anything that was missed.

Step 3: Switch roles

Set the timer again. Partner B speaks. Partner A mirrors.

Step 4: Reflect together

After both turns, discuss what the exercise felt like. Many couples notice that they interrupt more than they realize or that they often assume meaning before hearing the full story. The exercise slows communication down and strengthens understanding.

Practice this often. Even five minutes a week can shift the way you listen during everyday conversations.

SCRIPTS FOR SUPPORTIVE LISTENING

These simple scripts help you stay focused on understanding rather than reacting.

Script 1: Reflecting and confirming

What I hear you saying is, you felt alone handling everything today. Did I get that right.

Script 2: Inviting deeper sharing

Tell me more about what that felt like for you.

Use these sentences whenever conversations become emotional. They guide both partners back to connection.

Closing Thoughts

Listening is not a passive skill. It is an active choice to understand your partner's experience with care and attention. It requires setting aside your own reactions long enough to make room for their feelings. It requires patience, curiosity and humility. It requires presence.

When you listen to understand rather than to reply, you create a secure emotional bond. You help your partner feel valued and safe. You build trust. You create an atmosphere where difficult topics become easier to navigate.

If emotional safety is the foundation, listening is the structure that rises from that foundation. Without it, communication collapses. With it, love becomes stronger, steadier and more resilient.

In the next chapter, you will learn how to speak your needs in a clear and kind way that brings you closer instead of pushing you apart. Speaking and listening are partners. When you learn both, your conversations become a powerful source of connection.

Chapter 3
Speaking Your Needs Clearly and Kindly

Many relationship misunderstandings come from an invisible source. People have needs that they do not express clearly. Sometimes they do not express them at all. Sometimes they bury those needs under frustration, complaints or sarcasm. Sometimes they expect their partner to guess. Sometimes they fear that speaking honestly will start a conflict. When needs stay unspoken or unclear, resentment grows. Partners pull away instead of growing closer. Communication becomes tense, confusing or full of assumptions.

> Speaking needs clearly and kindly is one of the most important skills in a relationship.

When needs are expressed with honesty, calmness and respect, partners understand each other more easily. They respond with more care. They become more willing to meet each other in the middle. Needs that are spoken clearly create closeness. Needs that are hidden or expressed through blame create distance.

This chapter helps you understand why people struggle to express needs, how to distinguish needs from demands and how to speak in a way that brings your partner closer instead of pushing them away. You will learn a simple structure for expressing feelings without criticism and how to create conversations where both partners feel respected and understood.

Why People Hide Needs or Phrase Them as Complaints

It may seem surprising that something as natural as having needs can feel uncomfortable or risky. Yet many people grow up in environments where needs were ignored, punished or seen as burdens. Others develop habits of self reliance that make asking for anything feel vulnerable. Still others learn to communicate through hints or complaints because direct expression felt unsafe. Understanding these patterns helps you overcome them.

Here are the most common reasons people hide needs or turn them into complaints.

Fear of being rejected or ignored

Some people worry that if they express a need directly, their partner will say no or dismiss them. Avoiding rejection feels safer than facing it. So they hint, withdraw or use vague language. When the partner fails to respond to the hidden need, resentment grows.

Fear of conflict

Many people believe that asking for something will start an argument. They fear that their partner will react defensively or feel criticized. To avoid tension, they hold back their needs and hope things will improve on their own. This rarely works. Unspoken needs surface later as irritation.

Shame around needing too much

Some individuals believe they are too emotional, too sensitive or too demanding. This belief may come from past relationships or childhood experiences. They silence their needs to avoid feeling needy or burdensome. Over time this leads to loneliness even inside the relationship.

Habitual complaint communication

Complaints are indirect attempts to ask for something. Instead of saying I need more help with the laundry, a person says You never help with anything. Complaints are attempts to express unmet needs, but they come out wrapped in frustration. This creates defensiveness instead of understanding.

Expectation that partners should just know

Some people believe that if their partner truly loves them, they should be able to read their needs or feelings. This expectation sets both partners up for disappointment. Love does not give people mind reading abilities. Clarity is a gift that strengthens connection.

Not knowing the need beneath the emotion

Often people express irritation without understanding what they actually need. They say You are always late, but the deeper need is to feel respected and valued. They say You never listen, but the deeper need is to feel emotionally connected. Figuring out the true need creates communication that heals.

Past experiences where honesty did not feel safe

People carry emotional history into their relationships. If speaking needs led to punishment or ridicule in the past, the body remembers that fear. Even in a healthier relationship, the habit of staying silent can linger.

These reasons are human and normal. There is nothing wrong with you if speaking your needs feels vulnerable. The goal is not perfection. The goal is awareness and gentle growth.

The Difference Between Needs and Demands

Understanding the difference between a need and a demand is essential for healthy communication. Both involve wanting something. The difference lies in how they are expressed and how much space they give the other person.

What a need is

A healthy need is a request that invites connection. It expresses an emotional or practical desire while respecting the partner's autonomy. Needs are based on vulnerability and openness. They communicate what would help you feel loved, supported or understood.

Examples of healthy needs:

I need more quality time so I can feel connected to you.

I need reassurance when we go through stressful moments.

I need clearer communication about plans so I feel grounded.

I need affection to feel close.

A need is shared with the hope of being understood and supported. It leaves room for conversation and collaboration.

What a demand is

A demand is a rigid expectation backed by pressure, criticism or threat. It often arises from fear or frustration rather than vulnerability. Demands remove the partner's choice and create defensiveness.

Examples of demands:

You have to spend more time with me or else.

You better make more effort.

You need to stop doing that right now.

If you loved me you would do what I want.

Demands break emotional safety because they communicate control rather than connection.

How to tell the difference

Ask yourself these questions:

Does my tone invite conversation or pressure?

Am I sharing a vulnerable need or insisting on an outcome?

Is my partner free to respond honestly, or do they feel they must comply?

Am I open to hearing their needs too?

Healthy needs respect both partners. Demands try to force behavior. When you focus on expressing the heart of your need rather than controlling what happens, you create space for understanding and teamwork.

Why needs are not weaknesses

Some people believe that having needs makes them dependent or weak. In truth, needs are part of being human. Every person needs comfort, support, attention and affection. Expressing needs honestly builds connection. Hiding them builds walls.

> Needs invite love. Demands push love away.

How to Express Feelings Without Blame

When emotions rise, it is easy to slip into language that sounds blaming. Blame creates defensiveness. Defensiveness blocks understanding. Understanding disappears and the conversation becomes a conflict.

To speak effectively, you must express what you feel without attacking your partner's character or intentions. This requires awareness and structure.

Here is a simple approach that helps you communicate clearly and kindly.

Describe the situation without judgment

Start by stating what happened in a neutral way. Avoid words that imply intention or character flaws.

Instead of: You do not care about me.

Say: When you stayed on your phone while I was talking.

Instead of: You always ignore me.

Say: When you walked away in the middle of our conversation.

Neutral descriptions lower tension and help your partner stay open.

Name your feeling

Feelings are not accusations. They are inner experiences. Sharing them creates vulnerability and connection.

Examples:

I felt lonely.

I felt frustrated.

I felt sad.

I felt overwhelmed.

I felt unimportant.

Feelings open the door to understanding.

Identify the need beneath the feeling

Needs give meaning to feelings. They help your partner understand what would help you feel supported.

Examples:

I needed some reassurance.

I needed partnership.

I needed quality time.

I needed clarity.

I needed some help.

Make a specific request

Requests invite cooperation. They offer a path forward.

Examples:

Could we set aside fifteen minutes tonight to talk.

Could you check in with me when plans change.

Could you help with the dishes when I am stressed.

Requests communicate what would help rather than what is wrong.

Putting these pieces together creates a clear and kind statement.

The structure

When X happened, I felt Y, and what I need is Z.

This is simple, yet incredibly powerful. It promotes honesty without blame. It creates understanding rather than defensiveness. It invites your partner into your inner world.

Real examples

Example 1

When you raised your voice earlier, I felt anxious, and what I need is a slower and calmer pace so I can stay connected during disagreements.

Example 2

When you came home later than expected, I felt worried and then a little hurt. What I need is a quick message so I know what is going on.

Example 3

When you forgot the appointment, I felt overwhelmed because I had planned my schedule around it. What I need is a shared plan for remembering important dates.

None of these examples attack character. They focus on the speaker's experience. This invites empathy instead of argument.

How Tone and Timing Shape the Message

Even perfectly chosen words can land badly if the tone or timing is off. Emotional safety depends not only on what you say, but how and when you say it.

Use a calm tone

A gentle voice communicates care. A tense voice signals danger. Calm tones keep conversations open.

Choose a good moment

If your partner is stressed, exhausted or distracted, your message may not be received well. It is not avoidance to wait for a better moment. It is respect.

Try phrases like:

I want to talk about something important. When would be a good time.

I want us to feel calm when we talk about this.

Stay focused on your experience

Avoid the words always and never. These words exaggerate and usually lead to defensiveness.

Keep your message simple

One clear need is better than five tangled complaints. Focus on what matters most.

When tone and timing support your words, your partner is far more likely to respond with care.

When Needs Clash

Sometimes two partners have needs that seem to conflict. For example, one partner needs closeness during stress and the other needs space to think. One partner needs direct conversation while the other needs gentle pacing. These differences do not mean the relationship is incompatible. They simply mean both partners must share their needs clearly and work toward balance.

Here are the keys for handling conflicting needs:

Acknowledge both needs

Both needs are valid. Both deserve respect. When each partner feels heard, cooperation becomes easier.

Look for the deeper purpose

Often the needs have similar roots. One partner needs closeness for reassurance. The other needs space for emotional regulation. Both want connection. They simply reach it in different ways.

Collaborate on solutions

Ask questions such as:

How can we honor both of our needs.

What timing works for you.

What would help you feel supported and what would help me feel supported.

Be flexible

Healthy relationships adapt. Needs change as circumstances change. Stay open to adjusting.

Conflicting needs are not barriers. They are opportunities for teamwork.

How to Stay Kind While Speaking Your Needs

Speaking needs clearly does not mean being blunt or harsh. Kindness is essential. Kindness keeps communication safe. Kindness softens the message. Kindness opens your partner's heart rather than closing it.

Here are simple ways to keep kindness at the center.

Begin with connection

You can start by saying:

I care about us and want to talk about something.

My intention is connection, not conflict.

These openings set a reassuring tone.

Keep your voice gentle

A kind tone is more important than perfect wording.

Assume goodwill

Most misunderstandings come from differences in perception, not malice. Approach your partner with the belief that they want the relationship to work too.

Express appreciation when possible

You can say:

I know you have been trying.

I appreciate the effort you make.

Thank you for listening.

Appreciation strengthens cooperation.

Focus on the future, not past mistakes

Needs become easier to meet when the message is forward looking.

Speaking Needs During Conflict

It is hardest to speak kindly when you are upset. Yet conflict is when clear and respectful communication matters most. When emotions rise, pause and use structure to steady your words.

Here is a step by step method for speaking needs during conflict:

Step 1. Pause and breathe

Calm your body to prevent reactive statements.

Step 2. Identify your feeling

Ask yourself: What emotion am I truly experiencing. Hurt. Fear. Frustration. Loneliness.

Step 3. Identify the need beneath the feeling

Ask: What am I longing for in this moment. Understanding. Respect. Space. Comfort. Support.

Step 4. Speak with clarity

Use the phrase:

When X happened, I felt Y, and what I need is Z.

Step 5. Stay open to teamwork

Invite your partner into the solution.

How can we work through this together.

This approach turns conflict into connection.

When Your Partner Has Trouble Hearing Your Needs

Sometimes you express needs clearly, but your partner reacts poorly. They may feel blamed even when you are careful. They may shut down or defend themselves. They may feel overwhelmed or confused. This does not mean your needs are wrong. It means the conversation needs more emotional safety.

Here are ways to help your partner hear you:

Reassure them of your intention

Say:

I am not blaming you. I just want to share what is going on inside me.

This softens their defenses.

Slow the conversation down

Go slowly. Pause often. Let your partner process.

Invite their perspective

Say:

I want to hear your side too.

What was it like for you.

This turns the moment into collaboration.

Keep your tone gentle even if you are frustrated

Gentle delivery increases chances of understanding.

Ask for a better moment if emotions are high

A calm setting supports clarity.

When both partners feel safe, needs can be heard and understood.

Exercise: Turn One Complaint Into a Need Statement

This exercise helps you transform reactive communication into constructive communication.

Step 1: Write down a common complaint you have.

Examples:

You never listen.

You always leave me with the chores.

You do not care about my feelings.

Step 2: Identify the feeling beneath the complaint.

Are you hurt. Frustrated. Lonely. Overwhelmed. Unseen.

Step 3: Identify the need beneath the feeling.

Do you need reassurance. Partnership. Kindness. Attention. Clarity.

Step 4: Rewrite the complaint as a need statement using the structure.

When X happened, I felt Y, and what I need is Z.

Example transformation

Complaint: You never listen to me.

Need statement: When I am sharing something and you look at your phone, I feel unimportant. What I need is your full attention for a few minutes so I can feel connected.

Repeat this exercise often. Needs expressed clearly change relationships.

SCRIPTS FOR SPEAKING NEEDS KINDLY

These simple phrases guide you toward clarity and kindness.

Script 1: Structured need statement

When X happened, I felt Y, and what I need is Z.

Script 2: Reducing defensiveness

I am not blaming you. I just want to share what is going on inside me.

Use these scripts until they become natural.

Speaking your needs is an act of courage and care. It helps your partner understand you more deeply. It helps you build a relationship where honesty feels safe and vulnerability feels welcomed. Needs that are spoken clearly become bridges that bring partners closer. Needs that are hidden or expressed as complaints become barriers that push partners apart.

> You do not need perfect words. You only need sincerity, kindness and clarity.

When you express your needs respectfully, you create space for understanding and support. You give your partner a chance to show up for you. You strengthen emotional intimacy and trust.

Relationships thrive when both partners learn to speak openly and kindly about what matters to them. In the next chapter, you will explore emotional triggers and learn why small moments sometimes cause strong reactions. Understanding these triggers helps you speak and listen with even more compassion. Together, these skills form the foundation of deep and lasting connection.

Part 2

Understanding Patterns and Emotional Triggers

Chapter 4
Why You React the Way You Do

Every relationship contains moments that feel bigger than they should. A small comment feels sharp. A delayed text feels hurtful. A forgotten task feels disrespectful. A quiet sigh feels like rejection. When reactions come quickly and strongly, it may seem like your partner caused all the emotion. Yet most intense reactions have deeper origins. They come from emotional triggers and old stories that live inside us, often outside our awareness.

> Understanding your emotional triggers is not about blaming yourself. It is about seeing how past experiences shape present reactions so you can respond with more clarity and less fear.

It is about becoming aware of the patterns you bring into your relationship and learning how to share your inner world so your partner understands you better. When both partners understand their triggers, communication becomes gentler. Conflict becomes less personal. Connection becomes deeper.

This chapter explores why you react the way you do, how stress and fatigue influence your communication and how childhood experiences shape your emotional patterns. You will learn how to communicate about your inner world in ways that build closeness instead of confusion. You will discover how to pause before reacting and how to help your partner understand what is really happening inside you. With awareness and compassion, your emotional triggers can become sources of healing instead of sources of tension.

Emotional Triggers and Old Stories

An emotional trigger is a moment that activates a strong emotional reaction. The reaction often feels sudden and automatic. The trigger itself might be small, but it sets off a chain of internal responses that have been shaped by past experiences. These old experiences create emotional stories that influence how you interpret the present.

For example, if you grew up feeling unheard, a moment when your partner interrupts you can feel like dismissal. If you experienced unpredictability as a child, changes in plans can trigger anxiety or fear. If you learned to hide emotions to avoid conflict, seeing your partner upset might make your body tense even when the situation is not dangerous.

Emotional triggers are not flaws.

They are learned survival responses. Your mind and body adapted to earlier environments to keep you safe. The problem is that these protective responses sometimes activate in situations where you are actually secure and supported. When that happens, your reactions may feel outsized or confusing to both you and your partner.

Emotional triggers come in many forms. Here are some of the most common.

Tone of voice

A raised voice, a sigh or a shift in volume can remind you of past conflict or criticism. Even subtle changes can feel threatening if your nervous system learned to watch for danger.

Facial expressions

A frown, eye roll or blank expression can trigger feelings of fear, rejection or shame. These reactions often begin before your conscious mind has time to interpret them.

Feeling ignored or dismissed

Moments of feeling unheard can activate deep emotions if you once felt overlooked or invisible in childhood or past relationships.

Sudden changes in plans

Unpredictability can trigger old fears of instability, abandonment or lack of control.

Criticism or perceived criticism

Even gentle feedback can feel painful if earlier experiences associated criticism with rejection or lack of love.

Silence or withdrawal

When your partner goes quiet, it might remind you of earlier experiences where silence meant danger, punishment or emotional abandonment.

Closeness or affection

Even positive experiences can trigger fear if closeness once felt unsafe or uncertain.

These triggers do not reflect your partner's intentions. They reflect your history. When you understand that history, you gain power over your reactions.

How Triggers Shape Your Interpretation

When a trigger is activated, your brain moves quickly. It searches for meaning based on past experiences rather than present reality. You are not interpreting your partner. You are interpreting your own history.

For example:

If a parent or caretaker was unpredictable, you may interpret your partner's delayed response as abandonment instead of busyness.

If you were criticized harshly, you may interpret neutral feedback as attack.

If you learned to be perfect to avoid punishment, you may interpret small mistakes as catastrophic.

If you were taught to hide emotions, you may interpret your partner's tears as a sign you are failing rather than a sign they trust you enough to share.

Without awareness, these interpretations feel like truth instead of echoes. Recognizing this pattern allows you to step back and ask yourself whether your reaction belongs to the present or to the past.

How Stress and Fatigue Shape Reactions

You do not react only from your history. You also react from your current physical and emotional state. Stress and fatigue make reactions sharper and faster. When your body is tired or overwhelmed, it loses capacity for patience, empathy and thoughtful conversation.

Stress narrows your emotional bandwidth

Stress shifts your nervous system into a protective state. In this state, your body scans for danger, even in ordinary situations. This heightens sensitivity to tone, facial expression and wording. A calm conversation can suddenly feel tense because your body misreads signals through the lens of stress.

Fatigue reduces self regulation

When you are exhausted, your emotional self control weakens. You may snap quickly, shut down abruptly or struggle to choose kind words. This is not because you are uncaring. It is because your brain has fewer resources available for emotional processing.

Overload blocks listening

When you are overloaded, your ability to listen decreases. You respond more quickly, interrupt more often or drift away mentally. Your partner may interpret this as lack of interest when the real issue is emotional depletion.

Stress activates old emotional habits

Stress makes old patterns stronger. If you learned to withdraw, you may withdraw even faster. If you learned to defend yourself, you may react before thinking. Stress pushes the nervous system toward familiar coping strategies.

Stress distorts meaning

A stressed mind interprets neutral information negatively. A simple question like What happened today can sound like accusation. A partner's quietness can look like disapproval. The mind reads threat where none exists.

Fatigue reduces access to compassion

Compassion takes energy. When your energy is low, your emotional capacity shrinks. You may care deeply about your partner but feel unable to show it clearly.

When couples understand the effects of stress and fatigue, they become more patient with each other. They learn to ask whether a moment of tension comes from the relationship or from exhaustion. They recognize that physical and emotional states influence communication as much as words do.

How Childhood Learning Shapes Adult Reactions

Childhood experiences shape the templates we use in adult relationships. These templates include beliefs, expectations and emotional responses. Even positive childhood experiences can create rigid patterns that do not always serve us well. Understanding your early learning helps you break patterns that no longer fit your current relationship.

Here are some common childhood learning patterns and how they influence adult reactions.

Learning that emotions are dangerous

If you grew up in a home where anger, sadness or fear were punished or mocked, you may react strongly to emotional expression. You might feel unsafe when your partner shows emotion, even if they are not upset with you.

Learning to be the peacemaker

Some children learn that their role is to keep everyone calm. As adults, they may react with anxiety when conflict arises. They may rush to fix things immediately to avoid tension.

Learning that love is conditional

If love had to be earned through achievement, behavior or performance, you may react strongly to any sign of disappointment. Small feedback can feel like a threat to your worth.

Learning to suppress needs

If your needs were ignored or seen as inconvenient, you may feel uncomfortable expressing needs in adulthood. When needs arise, you might feel shame or guilt. You may also react strongly when you feel someone is disregarding you.

Learning that safety is unpredictable

If caretakers were inconsistent, your nervous system may be highly sensitive to unpredictability. A partner's late arrival or change in plans may trigger intense anxiety.

Learning that conflict meant danger

If conflict involved yelling, silence or instability in your childhood home, even mild disagreements may cause your body to tense. You might react by shutting down or trying to escape the conversation.

Learning to take care of others emotionally

Some children become emotional caretakers. As adults they may react strongly when partners seem upset because they feel responsible for fixing it. This pressure creates anxiety and reactive behavior.

Learning to be self sufficient

If you were expected to handle everything alone, needing support may feel unfamiliar or uncomfortable. When a partner offers help, you might react with irritation or discomfort because independence became a protective identity.

Recognizing these patterns helps you understand why certain moments strike emotional chords. It also helps you speak about your reactions with more compassion for yourself and your partner.

. . .

Helping Your Partner Understand Your Inner World

Your partner cannot see the emotional storms inside you unless you let them in. When you communicate how your history and current state influence your reactions, you give your partner a map to your emotional landscape. This creates greater empathy and reduces misinterpretation.

Here are the most effective ways to help your partner understand your inner world.

Speak from vulnerability rather than blame

Vulnerability invites connection. Blame creates defensiveness.

Instead of: You always make me feel this way.

Say: This reaction is bigger than the moment. Here is what it touches in me.

This communicates that your reaction comes from inside you, not from something inherently wrong with your partner.

Share the old story

Explain the childhood pattern or previous experience that influences your reaction.

For example:

I know I got reactive earlier. I grew up in a home where raised voices meant danger. Underneath my reaction was fear, not anger.

This helps your partner respond with empathy instead of confusion.

Describe the current emotion clearly

Your partner can support you better when they know what you are feeling. Describe your emotion in simple terms.

I felt rejected.

I felt overwhelmed.

I felt unimportant.

I felt scared.

Share what helps you calm down

Partners are often eager to help but do not know how. Give them guidance.

When I get triggered, it helps if you slow down and speak gently.

When I feel overwhelmed, it helps if you let me take a minute to breathe.

Invite your partner into a conversation, not a confession

You are not delivering a speech. You are building understanding. After sharing, ask:

Does that make sense.

What was that moment like for you.

How did it land when I reacted that way.

This turns the experience into a shared learning moment.

Own your reactions without shame

You can acknowledge your behavior while staying kind to yourself.

I know I reacted strongly. I see where it came from. I want to work on this.

This shows your partner that you are aware and committed to growth.

Encourage them to share their own inner world

Your honesty invites theirs. When both partners understand each other's triggers, misunderstandings decrease and compassion increases.

Rewriting the Story Through Awareness

Understanding your reactions does not mean you will never feel triggered again. Triggers are part of being human. What changes is your relationship to them. Instead of feeling swept away by a reaction, you learn to slow down and choose your response. You learn to breathe through the moment. You learn to speak about your feelings instead of letting them silently build.

                Awareness begins the healing process.

Each time you recognize an emotional trigger, you loosen its power. Each time you speak openly about your inner world, you strengthen trust. Each time your partner responds with empathy, your nervous system learns a new story. Over time, old triggers soften. The relationship becomes a safer place for emotions to unfold.

This process takes patience. It takes curiosity. It takes kindness. Yet the results are profound. Couples who learn to understand each other's triggers grow deeper intimacy. They handle conflict with more grace. They become gentler with each other because they know what the other person carries.

Exercise: Identify Three Flash Points and What They Are Really About

This exercise helps you understand your triggers more clearly and communicate them to your partner.

Step 1: Identify three flash points

Write down three situations that often trigger strong reactions for you. Examples:

When someone interrupts me.

When plans change suddenly.

When my partner seems upset.

When I feel ignored.

Step 2: Describe what happens inside you

For each flash point, describe your emotional and physical reaction. Do you feel tension. Do you get quiet. Do you raise your voice. Do you feel anxious or angry.

Step 3: Identify the old story behind the reaction

Ask yourself:

Does this remind me of something from childhood.

Does it resemble a past relationship experience.

What fear sits underneath the reaction.

Examples:

When plans change, it reminds me of unpredictability growing up.

When I feel ignored, it touches my fear of not being important.

When voices rise, it reminds me of past conflict that felt unsafe.

Step 4: Identify what you really need in those moments

Needs might include reassurance, clarity, space, gentleness or consistency.

Step 5: Share one flash point with your partner

Use gentle phrasing:

This reaction is bigger than the moment. Here is what it touches in me.

or

I know I got reactive. Here is what was underneath that.

This creates emotional connection and encourages your partner to share their own patterns.

Taylor Kade

SCRIPTS FOR COMMUNICATING ABOUT TRIGGERS

These scripts help you explain your reactions without blame.

Script 1: Highlighting the deeper history

This reaction is bigger than the moment. Here is what it touches in me.

Script 2: Owning your behavior with vulnerability

I know I got reactive. Here is what was underneath that.

Use these scripts to create understanding rather than conflict.

Your reactions are not random. They come from your history, your stress level, your emotional patterns and your human need for safety. When you understand why you react the way you do, you free yourself from confusion and guilt. You also free your partner from misinterpretation. Instead of seeing each other as difficult or over sensitive, you begin to see the emotional landscapes that shaped both of you.

> Understanding your triggers helps you slow
> down in moments of tension.

It helps you communicate with more clarity. It helps you speak from vulnerability instead of fear. It helps you build a relationship where emotional patterns become opportunities for closeness rather than sources of conflict.

In the next chapter, you will explore connection styles and learn how different emotional needs influence relationships. These insights will help you understand not only your own patterns but also your partner's, creating even more compassion and connection.

Chapter 5
The Three Connection Styles

Every person brings a unique style of connecting into their relationships. These styles influence how you communicate, how you show affection, how you react under stress and what you need to feel loved. They are not personality types. They are emotional patterns that come from a mix of childhood experiences, past relationships and natural temperament. Understanding these patterns helps couples speak with more compassion and respond to each other with greater sensitivity.

For the sake of clarity and simplicity, this chapter uses three connection styles that map onto common patterns found in long term relationships: reassurance seeking, space seeking and steady. These styles are not fixed categories. You may see yourself in more than one. Your style may shift depending on stress, life stage or partner. The goal is not to label yourself. The goal is to understand your emotional tendencies so you can communicate better and meet your partner in the middle.

> When partners understand each other's styles, conflict becomes easier to navigate. Misunderstandings decrease. Conversations become gentler.

Needs become clearer. Connection becomes stronger. This chapter explores how each style shows up, how each style communicates under stress and how couples with different styles can support each other.

Understanding the Three Connection Styles

Every style is a way of seeking safety, closeness or comfort. None of them are wrong. None of them are superior. Each style has strengths. Each style has challenges. When partners learn to accept and understand their own style, they become more grounded. When they learn to understand their partner's style, they become more loving.

Here are the three styles you will explore in this chapter.

Reassurance Seeking Style

People with this style tend to seek closeness and clarity during stress. They feel safer when emotional connection is clear and consistent. When conversations become tense, they usually want to talk sooner rather than later. They may become anxious when they sense distance. They may interpret silence as withdrawal. They often worry about losing connection or being misunderstood. Their longing for closeness is not clinginess. It is an attempt to restore emotional safety.

Strengths of this style include emotional sensitivity, strong empathy and a desire for honest communication. Challenges include difficulty tolerating uncertainty, tendency to assume the worst and moments of urgency during conflict.

Space Seeking Style

People with this style tend to regulate their emotions by stepping back during stress. They feel safer when they have time to think, breathe and process quietly. When conversations become intense, they often need a pause. They may shut down or go quiet when overwhelmed. They do not withdraw because they do not care. They withdraw because their emotions feel too large or too confusing to handle in the moment.

Strengths of this style include calmness, logical thinking and ability to de escalate when grounded. Challenges include difficulty staying present in emotional moments, tendency to avoid vulnerability and patterns of withdrawal that their partner may misinterpret as disinterest.

Steady Style

People with this style tend to stay balanced during stress. They are generally comfortable with closeness and independence. They are usually patient listeners and clear communicators. They value connection but do not feel overwhelmed by distance. They can be supportive during conflict without becoming overly reactive or withdrawn.

Strengths of this style include stability, reliability and emotional balance. Challenges include occasional difficulties understanding the intensity of the other styles, or sometimes seeming too neutral when deeper emotion is needed.

Most couples contain a mix of these styles. The most common dynamic is one partner who seeks reassurance and another who seeks space. This dynamic often creates tension until both partners understand that their reactions are driven by emotional patterns, not by lack of love.

How Each Style Talks Under Stress

Communication changes dramatically when partners feel stressed, tired or emotionally activated. Understanding how each style communicates under stress can help you recognize patterns in your relationship and respond with greater empathy.

Here is how the three styles typically talk when they feel overwhelmed.

Reassurance Seeking Style Under Stress

When this style feels threatened, the need for connection becomes intense. They want to talk immediately. They need clarity. They want reassurance that everything is still stable. Their words may come quickly. Their tone may carry urgency. Their questions may feel repetitive because they are trying to soothe their own anxiety.

Common communication signs:

Asking, Are we okay.

Seeking immediate resolution.

Wanting to revisit the conversation again and again.

Expressing worries about distance or disconnection.

Taking a partner's silence personally.

Intensifying efforts to get attention or understanding.

When this style does not receive reassurance, their anxiety increases. Their mind starts imagining worst case scenarios. They may criticize or raise concerns more directly in order to get a response. They are not trying to attack. They are trying to feel safe.

What they are truly saying underneath the words is:

Please connect with me. I feel scared. I need to know we are okay.

Space Seeking Style Under Stress

When this style feels threatened, the need for distance increases. Their emotions feel overwhelming. They need time alone to regulate. They may become quiet, distant or slow to respond. This is not rejection. It is self protection. Their mind becomes overloaded and they cannot hear or think clearly until they calm down.

Common communication signs:

Giving short responses.

Looking away or withdrawing physically.

Wanting to leave the room.

Saying I do not know when asked emotional questions.

Avoiding eye contact.

Shutting down when the conversation becomes intense.

When this style does not receive the space they need, they may become defensive or irritated. They may feel trapped. They may feel like they are failing or disappointing their partner. They may become quieter until they emotionally shut off.

What they are truly saying underneath the withdrawal is:

I care about you, but I feel overwhelmed. I need space so I do not shut down completely.

Steady Style Under Stress

This style usually tries to stay calm. They may attempt to mediate or smooth the interaction. They may slow the conversation and encourage both partners to breathe. They are often good at seeing multiple perspectives and try to keep the conversation balanced.

Common communication signs:

Using calm or neutral tone even when upset.

Trying to problem solve once emotions stabilize.

Asking questions like What do you need right now.

Offering reassurance without becoming overwhelmed.

Pausing to think before responding.

Challenges arise when the steady partner misunderstands the emotional intensity of the other styles. They may underestimate how scared or overwhelmed their partner feels.

They may try to be rational when their partner needs emotional presence.

What they are truly saying underneath their calmness is:

I want to help. I want us to stay grounded. I am here with you.

Where Misunderstandings Begin

> Misunderstandings often happen when one partner tries to meet their own emotional needs without realizing that their behavior triggers the other style.

For example:

A reassurance seeking partner reaches for connection, but the space seeking partner feels overwhelmed and pulls away.

The more the reassurance seeker reaches, the more the space seeker withdraws.

The more the space seeker withdraws, the more the reassurance seeker reaches.

This creates a cycle that feels painful for both.

The reassurance seeking partner thinks:

Why are you pulling away. Do you not care about me.

The space seeking partner thinks:

Why are you coming closer. I need a minute to breathe.

Both are reacting from patterns, not from lack of love.

Understanding these patterns helps couples break the cycle.

How to Meet Each Other in the Middle

When couples understand each other's styles, they can create new patterns that support both partners. Meeting in the middle means respecting each person's emotional needs while finding solutions that work for the relationship.

Here is how each style can adjust and support the others.

If you have a reassurance seeking style

Your strengths are emotional awareness, openness and desire for closeness. These strengths help relationships thrive. Your challenge is tolerating uncertainty long enough for your partner to stay grounded.

Here is how to meet your partner in the middle:

Slow your pace when your partner is overwhelmed

Fast talking increases pressure. Pause. Breathe. Allow silence.

Ask for reassurance without attacking

Instead of saying You never listen, say I need to feel connected right now.

Allow your partner to take short breaks

Breaks are not abandonment. They are regulation tools.

Trust that distance does not equal rejection

Give your partner time to return.

Notice catastrophic thinking

Ask yourself whether your fear comes from the present or from past experiences.

When you slow your approach, your partner can stay open instead of shutting down.

If you have a space seeking style

Your strengths are calmness, patience and ability to create emotional stability. Your challenge is staying present long enough to show that you care.

Here is how to meet your partner in the middle:

Communicate when you need space instead of withdrawing silently

Say: I care and I just need a pause. I will come back in ten minutes.

Give reassurance even while taking space

Even a simple sentence like I am here for you helps your partner feel safer.

Return when you say you will

Returning builds trust. It shows that your pause was for regulation, not avoidance.

Share your internal experience

Tell your partner what overwhelms you and why.

Practice small doses of emotional presence

You do not need to stay in long emotional conversations. You only need to stay long enough to show care.

When you communicate more clearly, your partner feels supported rather than abandoned.

If you have a steady style

Your strengths are balance, patience and reliability. Your challenge is remembering that other styles feel emotions more intensely.

Here is how to meet your partner in the middle:

Offer emotional language, not just logical solutions

Your partner may need to hear I understand how hard that was.

Check in more often than you think you need to

Small reassurances go a long way.

Validate emotional experiences even when they seem intense

Intensity is not a flaw. It is a reaction to a felt threat.

Share more of your inner world

Some steady partners under share. Be open about your feelings.

Do not rush the conversation toward resolution

Stay with the emotion for a moment before thinking of solutions.

Meeting in the middle helps couples feel balanced and connected.

How Mixed Style Couples Can Thrive

Most couples have different styles. This is not a problem. It is an opportunity. When partners learn how to collaborate instead of reacting, they create a relationship that blends the strengths of both styles.

Here is how mixed style couples can support each other.

Practice the pause and return method

The reassurance seeking partner allows the pause.

The space seeking partner commits to returning at a specific time.

Both get what they need: space and reassurance.

Use bridging sentences

Bridging sentences help both partners stay regulated.

Reassurance seeker:

I need connection, but I can give you a few minutes.

Space seeker:

I need space, but I am staying with you and will return soon.

Create predictable patterns

Predictability helps both styles feel safe.

This may include regular check ins, clarifying plans or setting communication agreements during conflict.

Celebrate strengths

Reassurance seekers bring emotional depth.

Space seekers bring calm.

Steady partners bring balance.

Together they create a flexible, resilient team.

Talk openly about your needs

Honesty prevents misinterpretation. When partners speak clearly about what they need, they reduce fear and build trust.

Exercise: A Short Quiz to Recognize Your Patterns

This quiz helps you identify your primary connection style. Choose the answers that feel most true for you in everyday life and under stress.

Question 1: When conflict begins, I usually want to

A. Talk immediately and resolve things.

B. Step back and gather my thoughts.

C. Stay calm and understand both sides.

Question 2: When my partner feels distant, I usually feel

A. Anxious or unsettled.

B. Relieved to have space.

C. Curious but not overwhelmed.

Question 3: When I am stressed, I usually

A. Reach for reassurance.

B. Withdraw or shut down.

C. Stay steady and try to remain balanced.

Question 4: What I need most during conflict is

A. Connection and clarity.

B. Space and time to think.

C. Calm conversation.

Question 5: My partner sometimes says I

A. Need too much reassurance.

B. Pull away when things get hard.

C. Seem neutral or too calm.

Scoring

Mostly A: Reassurance seeking style.

Mostly B: Space seeking style.

Mostly C: Steady style.

A mix: You are flexible and influenced by context. That is normal.

Use your results to help you understand your tendencies and to communicate your needs with greater clarity.

SCRIPTS FOR SUPPORTING EACH CONNECTION STYLE

These scripts are simple yet powerful. They help couples respond to each other with kindness and emotional awareness.

For reassurance seeking partners

I am here and I am not going anywhere. Let us slow this down.

For space seeking partners

I care and I just need a pause. I will come back in ten minutes.

Use them regularly until they become natural.

Connection styles shape the rhythms of your relationship. They influence how you seek comfort, how you deal with conflict and how you communicate your feelings. When you understand your style, you gain insight into your emotional patterns. When you understand your partner's style, you gain compassion for their reactions.

Differences in styles are not problems. They are opportunities for growth. They help you learn patience, flexibility and deeper emotional intelligence. When couples master the art of meeting in the middle, their connection becomes stronger, their communication becomes clearer and their relationship becomes more resilient.

In the next chapter, you will explore how to turn conflict into collaboration by understanding the cycles that pull couples apart and learning new habits that bring them back together.

Chapter 6
Turning Conflict Into Collaboration

Conflict is not a sign that a relationship is failing. Conflict is a sign that two people care enough to be affected by each other. Every couple argues. Every couple gets frustrated. Every couple has misunderstandings. What separates strong couples from struggling ones is not the presence of conflict. It is how the conflict is handled.

> Healthy conflict leads to deeper understanding, stronger trust and clearer communication.

Unhealthy conflict leads to looping arguments, emotional distance and resentment. The goal is not to eliminate conflict. The goal is to transform conflict into collaboration. When partners learn how to slow arguments, listen with presence and repair moments of tension, they turn conflict into a doorway for closeness rather than disconnection.

This chapter explores why couples get stuck in looping fights, how to slow arguments before they escalate and how to repair with skill rather than waiting for a perfect moment. It also teaches you how to map conflict patterns so you can break them together. With these tools, conflict becomes less frightening and more manageable, creating a relationship where differences can bring partners closer instead of driving them apart.

Why Couples Get Stuck in Looping Fights

Looping fights are arguments that repeat the same pattern over and over. The topic may change, but the emotional cycle stays the same. Both partners feel stuck. Hidden fears and unmet needs drive the cycle, but neither person realizes what is fueling it. The conversation becomes less about the issue and more about the emotions underneath.

Here are the most common reasons couples get trapped in looping fights.

Emotional activation happens faster than understanding

When conflict begins, the body reacts before the mind has time to think. Heart rate increases. Breathing speeds up. Muscles tense. The nervous system shifts into protection mode. In this state, people misunderstand tone, assume negative intentions and listen through a filter of fear. Arguments escalate quickly because both partners are reacting rather than understanding.

Partners argue about symptoms instead of roots

Most conflicts are not about the surface issue. They are about deeper needs such as respect, appreciation, safety, attention or support. When couples argue about dishes, schedules or chores, they are often really arguing about feeling alone, unimportant, unheard or overwhelmed. Because the true need is hidden, the argument cannot resolve fully. So it repeats.

Opposite conflict styles collide

Often one partner wants to talk immediately to feel close, while the other needs space to process. The more one pushes for connection, the more the other withdraws. The more one withdraws, the more the other intensifies their efforts. The loop becomes self sustaining.

Each partner tries to prove their version of events

Arguments escalate when partners try to win. They list evidence, correct details, defend their intentions and argue about who is right. The conversation becomes a courtroom instead of a collaboration.

Past hurts leak into present moments

When old grievances are not fully healed, they rise up quickly during new conflicts. Something small reminds one partner of an earlier disappointment, and they react strongly. The other partner feels confused or attacked because the reaction seems disproportionate. The past becomes part of the present argument without naming it.

Partners expect the other to read their mind

Hidden expectations fuel looping fights. A partner may expect the other to know when they are overwhelmed, hurt or lonely. When that expectation is not met, frustration builds. The partner reacts strongly, but the other does not know what they did wrong, so they defend themselves. Both feel misunderstood.

Each partner focuses on their own pain

When conflict arises, it is natural to focus on your own hurt. But when both partners focus only on their own experience, empathy disappears. Without empathy, conflict becomes a struggle for emotional survival. Partners speak louder, faster or sharper. The argument loops because neither feels seen.

Understanding these patterns is the first step in breaking them. Looping fights lose power when partners focus on shared understanding instead of proving a point.

How to Slow Arguments Before They Escalate

Arguments escalate quickly because the body moves into threat mode. When partners learn to slow the early moments of conflict, they prevent the emotional spiral that makes resolution difficult. Slowing conflict is not about ignoring problems. It is about protecting the relationship while addressing the issue.

Here are the most effective ways to slow arguments before they escalate.

Notice the early signs

Arguments rarely explode out of nowhere. There are early warning signs that tell you tension is rising.

Common signs include:

Faster heartbeat

Raised voice

Shorter responses

Interrupting

Feeling misunderstood

Feeling criticized

Feeling disrespected

Wanting to walk away

Feeling the need to prove your point

When you notice these early signs, pause. You are catching the argument before it becomes too intense.

Name what is happening

Naming the tension reduces its power. You can say:

I want us to pause. I am starting to feel tense.

I can feel myself getting overwhelmed. Can we slow this down.

Naming the moment signals to your partner that you want connection, not conflict. It transforms the atmosphere immediately.

Shift from reaction to intention

Before responding, ask yourself:

What is my intention right now.

Do I want to understand, or do I want to win.

Do I want connection, or do I want to protect myself.

When partners shift their intention toward understanding, the conversation becomes gentler.

Lower your voice

Soft voices calm nervous systems. When you lower your voice, your partner's body interprets the moment as safer. They are more likely to listen without becoming defensive.

Use slowing phrases

Phrases that slow the emotional pace include:

Let us take a moment.

I want to understand you.

Let us breathe for a second.

I want us to stay connected while we talk about this.

Can we start again but slower.

These phrases signal teamwork instead of opposition.

Take brief, structured pauses

A short break can prevent escalation. The key is to make the break intentional rather than reactive.

You can say:

I need five minutes to settle myself. I will come back to you.

I care about this conversation, and I want to have it calmly. Let me pause for a moment.

Breaks allow both partners to reset rather than shut down.

Bring curiosity into the conversation

Curiosity is the antidote to conflict. Ask questions that help you understand your partner's feelings rather than defend your own.

Questions like:

What felt important about that moment for you.

What were you hoping for.

What did I miss.

Curiosity softens tension by shifting the focus from conflict to understanding.

Remember the goal is connection

Arguments escalate when partners forget that they are on the same side. A simple grounding phrase like I am on your team can stop an argument from spiraling.

When you keep connection at the center, communication becomes more respectful and constructive.

The Role of the Nervous System in Conflict

Emotions live in the body as much as the mind. During conflict, the nervous system becomes alert. It prepares you to fight, flee or freeze. This protective system helped humans survive danger but complicates modern relationships.

Here is how the nervous system influences conflict:

Fight response

You raise your voice, argue, interrupt or become confrontational. You are trying to protect yourself by pushing back.

Flight response

You withdraw, shut down, avoid eye contact or leave the room. You are trying to protect yourself by escaping the emotional threat.

Freeze response

You become quiet, numb or stuck. You cannot think clearly or access your feelings.

Understanding these responses reduces shame. You are not being dramatic. You are reacting from biology. When partners learn to recognize these states, they become more compassionate. They understand that their partner is not trying to hurt them. They are trying to protect themselves.

Why Slowing Conflict Creates Space for Understanding

When you slow the early moments of conflict, you create emotional space. Emotional space allows:

clearer thinking

deeper listening

softer tone

more empathy

more patience

less defensiveness

Slowing the pace allows both partners to hear the feelings beneath the words. It prevents misinterpretations. It gives the nervous system time to settle. It helps partners stay connected while working through differences.

Slowing conflict is a gift you offer to each other. It protects the relationship from emotional harm and builds trust.

Repair as a Skill, Not a Magic Moment

Many people believe that repair happens automatically. They expect time to fix hurt feelings. They hope that if enough hours pass, the tension will disappear. But time alone rarely repairs emotional wounds. Repair is a skill. A learned behavior. A conscious action.

Repair means returning to your partner after a moment of tension and rebuilding connection. It means taking responsibility for your part of the conflict. It means acknowledging your partner's feelings. It means expressing care. Repair is an active choice to protect the relationship even when emotions were difficult.

Couples who repair well stay close. Couples who skip repair grow distant. Even small ruptures, when left unrepaired, accumulate into resentment. The goal is not perfection. The goal is consistent repair.

Here is what repair requires.

Awareness of your own part

You do not need to take full blame. You only need to acknowledge the role you played.

You might say:

I see that my tone came out sharp.

I know I reacted quickly.

I should have slowed down before responding.

These statements show accountability without shame.

Acknowledgment of your partner's experience

Your partner may feel hurt, dismissed, overwhelmed or unseen. Acknowledging their experience validates their feelings.

Examples:

I see that my reaction made you feel small.

I understand that you felt ignored when I walked away.

I hear that my words hurt you even though I did not intend them to.

Validation helps your partner feel understood.

Reassurance about your intention

Reassurance repairs emotional safety.

Examples:

You matter to me.

I care about us.

I want to work through this together.

I am committed to understanding you.

Reassurance rebuilds trust.

Sharing your internal experience

When you explain what was happening inside you, your partner understands you more clearly.

Examples:

I reacted because I got scared.

I shut down because I felt overwhelmed.

My frustration came from stress, not from lack of love.

Sharing internal experience turns misunderstanding into clarity.

Expressing what you want to do differently

Repair includes forward movement.

Examples:

Next time I will tell you when I need a pause.

I want to work on speaking more gently.

I want to slow the conversation earlier.

These commitments show that you are not repeating old patterns.

Inviting your partner to share

Repair is not a monologue. It is a conversation.

You can say:

I want to hear your experience too.

How did that moment feel for you.

This opens the door for mutual understanding.

Offering warmth and affection when appropriate

Physical affection, a gentle tone or a soft smile can help integrate the repair emotionally, as long as your partner is receptive.

Why Repair Matters More Than Perfection

Partners will make mistakes. They will misunderstand each other. They will react in ways they regret. Mistakes do not harm relationships. Unrepaired mistakes do.

Repair sends a message:

Our connection matters more than this argument.

We can come back from difficult moments.

We can trust each other to care about the relationship.

Repair builds resilience. It creates a relationship where partners feel safe to be imperfect because they know they can reconnect.

Exercise: Conflict De Escalation Map

This exercise helps you identify your conflict patterns and create a plan for slowing and repairing conflict together.

Step 1: Identify your escalation signals

Write down the physical, emotional and behavioral signs that show you are getting activated.

Examples:

heart rate rising

interrupting

short replies

withdrawal

feeling the urge to prove a point

Step 2: Identify your partner's escalation signals

Write down what you notice when your partner becomes overwhelmed.

Examples:

quieter tone

more rapid talking

looking away

more intense questioning

defensiveness

Step 3: Identify the moment of no return

This is the point where the argument starts to loop.

Examples:

when voices rise

when one partner leaves the room

when someone starts correcting details

when needs turn into accusations

Step 4: Create a pause plan

Together choose phrases and actions that help pause the conflict.

Examples:

I want us to pause. I am on your team.

Let us take a minute to breathe.

I need a short break but I will come back.

Step 5: Create a repair ritual

Decide how you will reconnect after a difficult moment.

Examples:

Each partner shares their internal experience.

Each partner acknowledges one thing they understand better.

Each partner expresses one forward focused desire.

This map becomes a shared tool for staying connected through conflict.

SCRIPTS FOR COLLABORATIVE CONFLICT

These scripts help couples shift out of adversarial roles and into teamwork.

Script for slowing conflict

I want us to pause. I am on your team.

Script for finding shared goals

Let us find the part of this we both want.

These scripts remind both partners that they are allies, not opponents.

Conflict is not the enemy of love. Avoiding conflict does not create closeness. What creates closeness is the ability to understand each other during conflict, slow the pace before emotions overwhelm the conversation, and repair with intention afterward.

When couples learn to turn conflict into collaboration, they build a relationship that grows stronger through challenges rather than weaker. They stop fearing conflict and start using it as an opportunity for deeper understanding. They develop trust that even difficult moments can bring them closer.

Slowing arguments, communicating with empathy and repairing with care are not signs of weakness. They are signs of emotional maturity and relational strength. They are the habits of couples who stay connected for years.

In the next chapter, you will learn how daily connection habits create emotional warmth and prevent conflict from taking root in the first place.

Part 3

Conversations That Build Closeness

Chapter 7
Daily Connection Habits

Connection is the quiet heartbeat of every strong relationship. It is not created through dramatic moments or impressive declarations. It is built through daily habits of presence and care. These habits are often small, sometimes barely noticeable from the outside, but they have powerful effects on how two people feel about each other over time.

> When connection is nurtured daily, couples feel secure, valued and supported.

When connection fades, even couples who deeply love each other can begin to feel like strangers sharing responsibilities rather than partners sharing life.

Daily connection habits create a sense of emotional reliability. They communicate that even when life is chaotic, the relationship remains a stable and nurturing place. These habits prevent emotional distance from growing. They make conflict easier to resolve because emotional warmth softens the impact of misunderstandings. They make the relationship feel alive rather than routine.

Many couples assume connection requires long conversations, date nights or big gestures. Those experiences are wonderful, but they are not the foundation. The foundation is built from how you greet each other in the morning, how you talk during busy days, how you reunite after being apart and how you close the day together. These moments shape how safe and valued you feel with each other.

This chapter explores simple habits that fit into even the busiest schedules. These habits are not heavy, complicated or time intensive. They take minutes, yet they sustain emotional closeness in powerful ways. You will learn how small routines shape the nervous system, how appreciation shifts the emotional climate and how micro intimacy keeps partners connected even when life demands much of them.

Love grows where attention lives. Daily connection is how you give that attention.

Six Minute Connection Routines

Six minutes a day can strengthen a relationship more than an occasional two hour date night. Love thrives in consistency. Even brief moments of connection regulate stress, increase emotional attunement and remind partners that they are important to each other. These routines create emotional continuity throughout the day, preventing disconnect that often builds during busy seasons.

Below are six simple routines that can transform the emotional atmosphere of a relationship. None require planning. All require intention.

One minute morning check in

The first moments of the day set the emotional tone for everything that follows. A one minute morning check in helps partners feel oriented toward each other rather than immediately pulled into tasks, messages or responsibilities.

You can use this moment to pause, breathe and acknowledge each other. This moment says, You matter to me. I see you. You are part of my day.

Examples include:

How did you sleep.

Is there something you are looking forward to today.

Is there anything you feel anxious about that I can support.

I am glad to start my morning with you.

These moments soothe the nervous system and create an emotional anchor for the day. They remind partners that they are teammates before they are task managers. Even if mornings are rushed, a quick moment of connection creates warmth that carries forward.

One minute midday touch point

Midday can feel long and disconnected, especially if one or both partners are dealing with stress. A quick connection touch point breaks the emotional distance that naturally forms throughout the day. Even a brief message can renew closeness.

Examples:

Thinking of you.

Hope your day is going alright.

Just a small hello because you crossed my mind.

Sending you a little encouragement.

These messages do not need depth. They simply need presence. The purpose is not conversation. The purpose is reassurance. You are letting your partner know that you remain connected even when apart. This strengthens the bond and reduces misunderstandings later.

Two minute evening wind down

Evenings often carry emotional weight. Each partner brings home their stress, fatigue and stories from the day. Without intentional connection, evenings can slip into parallel routines where partners coexist without truly engaging. A simple two minute check in prevents this drift.

This check in uses two questions:

What was one good moment of your day.

What was one hard moment of your day.

These questions create a safe space for emotional sharing. They help each partner feel known. They also reveal small stresses or small joys that might not otherwise get attention.

A good moment may be a quiet cup of coffee. A hard moment may be a frustrating meeting. Sharing these small pieces helps both partners stay attuned to each other's emotional world. It prevents silent stress from turning into irritability or misunderstanding later in the evening.

Two minute bedtime closeness

Ending the day with connection builds a sense of emotional security. The brain remembers how interactions end more strongly than how they begin. A gentle moment at bedtime supports better sleep, lowers stress and deepens intimacy.

Bedtime connection can include:

a slow cuddle

a brief appreciation

a sentence of reassurance

a few calm breaths together

a hand placed lovingly on the other's back or arm

You might say:

I appreciate how you handled things today.

I am grateful for you.

Thank you for being my partner.

I love ending the day with you.

These small closings create a stable emotional rhythm. Even if the day was difficult, bedtime becomes a place of reconnection.

Weekly weekend reset

Once a week, choose a few minutes to check in about the relationship itself. This ritual creates stability in long term communication. It prevents small misunderstandings from accumulating unnoticed.

Your weekend reset can include:

What went well for us this week.

What felt challenging.

Is there anything one of us needs more support with.

What could make next week feel smoother.

These questions help couples stay aligned. They promote teamwork. They also show that the relationship deserves regular attention, not only emergency attention.

Mini repair and re connect moment

Effort in relationships does not eliminate conflict. What matters is repair. A mini repair moment can happen in under two minutes and can prevent emotional distance from forming.

Examples:

I am sorry for the tension earlier. I want to reconnect.

I see my part and I care about you.

I want us to feel close again.

Can we reset together.

Small repairs teach your nervous system that conflict does not threaten the relationship. This increases emotional safety and reduces future arguments.

Why Six Minute Habits Work

These habits work because they support the nervous system. Human connection releases calming chemicals that reduce stress hormones and increase feelings of safety. When couples connect frequently, even briefly, their bodies learn to relax with each other. This reduces tension, softens communication and strengthens resilience.

These routines also counteract the modern tendency toward distraction. They create intentional moments that remind partners to look up from their devices, turn toward each other and remember the shared emotional world between them.

Connection is not measured by time. It is measured by consistency and presence.

Appreciation and Micro Intimacy

Micro intimacy consists of small, spontaneous gestures that communicate love without requiring effort or planning. These gestures maintain warmth and help partners feel valued. They support emotional connection in both subtle and powerful ways.

Appreciation is one of the most important forms of micro intimacy. It removes the emotional fog that often builds in long term relationships where responsibilities overshadow tenderness. Appreciation highlights what is working rather than what is lacking. It invites gratitude instead of criticism.

Here are forms of micro intimacy that keep relationships alive.

Spoken appreciation

Daily appreciation changes the emotional climate of a relationship. It reduces defensiveness, increases generosity and encourages positive behavior.

A simple daily script can be:

One thing I appreciated about you today was...

This can include large actions or small gestures. The important part is noticing and naming.

Examples:

I appreciated how patient you were with the kids.

I appreciated that you made time for us.

I appreciated how you listened earlier.

I appreciated your sense of humor today.

Appreciation nourishes emotional connection.

Affectionate micro touch

Micro touch includes small, affectionate gestures that take seconds but carry emotional weight. These gestures say, I feel close to you.

Examples:

a hand on the arm

a brief shoulder squeeze

a small kiss

touching feet under a blanket

resting your head on your partner's shoulder

Physical closeness regulates the nervous system. It communicates love without words. Even touch that lasts one second can create warmth.

Shared smiles

A quick smile creates emotional resonance. It communicates fondness. It reminds your partner that they matter.

Smiles work even during tension. They soften the atmosphere and create possibility. They communicate that the relationship remains intact even when emotions rise.

. . .

Inside jokes and shared memories

Inside jokes create a private emotional world between partners. They remind you that your relationship is unique. They build a sense of us.

Shared memories can be revived by a simple sentence like:

Remember that time we...

These conversations rebuild emotional pathways of closeness.

Words of encouragement

Supportive words help partners feel safe and valued. They do not need to be dramatic.

Examples:

You are doing great.

I am proud of you.

I believe in you.

I see how hard you are trying.

I am with you.

Encouragement builds emotional strength in the relationship.

Acts of thoughtfulness

Small helpful actions create micro intimacy.

Examples:

bringing your partner a glass of water

sending a supportive message

turning down the bed

making coffee

taking over a small task when they are tired

Thoughtful actions make partners feel cared for without being asked.

Softened tone and gentle transitions

How you speak matters as much as what you say. A gentle tone communicates kindness. A softened transition, such as placing a hand on your partner before bringing up a topic, signals that connection matters.

These micro moments create a relational environment where both partners feel safe.

How to Stay Close Even When Schedules Are Chaotic

Connection often weakens not because love disappears but because life becomes overwhelming. Work demands, parenting, health issues, long commutes and emotional stress can disrupt communication. When partners are tired and pulled in multiple directions, closeness becomes the first thing to slip.

Here are ways to stay close even when life is chaotic.

Prioritize small moments, not big plans

Grand gestures are difficult during busy seasons. Small gestures are always possible. Use natural transitions to connect: greeting one another warmly, offering a quick kiss, sharing a moment of eye contact.

A thirty second moment can feel like a lifeline when schedules are full.

Let your partner into your internal world

When life is overwhelming, share your feelings even if briefly. Let your partner know if you are drained, anxious or stretched thin. This prevents misunderstandings and invites support.

Examples:

I am tired today, but I still want to connect for a minute.

I am overwhelmed, but I do not want to be distant.

This builds emotional closeness even during stress.

Protect short connection windows

Identify a few guaranteed daily windows and guard them. This could be a morning moment, five minutes after work, or bedtime closeness. These windows become anchors that prevent emotional drift.

Reduce unnecessary distractions

Phones and screens limit presence. Choose a few device free moments each day. Even five minutes of focused attention can transform connection.

Share tasks and emotional load

Lightening each other's responsibilities increases emotional availability. When practical burdens decrease, emotional energy increases.

Speak directly about wanting connection

Many couples wait for the perfect moment to reconnect. Instead, speak your desire openly.

Examples:

I miss you.

Can we make space for each other today.

I want to feel close.

Direct communication prevents silent assumptions.

Use rituals to create stability

Rituals bring predictability to chaotic schedules. Weekly breakfasts, evening appreciation practices or weekend resets help couples stay emotionally grounded.

Barriers to Daily Connection

Even with good intentions, couples face obstacles. Here is how to work through them.

Fatigue

When tired, emotional presence becomes difficult. Keep habits small and manageable. Even thirty seconds of presence matters.

Stress overload

Stress can lead to irritability or withdrawal. Naming your stress helps your partner understand your state without taking it personally.

Feeling unnoticed

If you feel unappreciated, connection becomes harder. Speak your feelings kindly and request more appreciation.

Phone habits

Technology steals connection. Create micro agreements to limit device use during key moments.

Differences in emotional energy

Partners rarely have the same desire for closeness. Compromise helps. Keep core routines small so both can sustain them.

Forgetting

Routines prevent forgetting. Tie connection habits to existing daily actions like brushing teeth or making coffee.

Exercise: Create a Weekly Ritual of Connection

This exercise helps you design a ritual that keeps your relationship steady and supported.

Step 1: Select a day and time

Choose a predictable window each week.

Step 2: Choose the purpose

Clarify whether the ritual is for emotional check in, planning, appreciation or relaxation.

Step 3: Choose the structure

Examples include:

two appreciations each

one stress and one joy from the week

a plan for upcoming challenges

a moment of affection or warmth

Step 4: Keep it simple and enjoyable

Short and light encourages consistency.

Step 5: Revisit and refine

Adapt the ritual as needed.

Rituals provide emotional continuity even in chaotic seasons.

SCRIPTS FOR DAILY CONNECTION

Script 1: Daily appreciation

One thing I appreciated about you today was...

Script 2: Emotional check in

What was one good moment and one hard moment of your day.

Use these scripts often. Their simplicity is part of their effectiveness.

Closing Thoughts

Daily connection habits are the quiet power behind lasting love. They transform ordinary days into shared emotional experiences. They strengthen trust, prevent misunderstandings and deepen intimacy. Relationships flourish when partners choose presence over distraction, gratitude over assumption and small moments of closeness over emotional avoidance.

Connection is not a feeling. It is a practice. When you commit to these habits, your relationship becomes a place of warmth, steadiness and joy, even during the busiest seasons of life.

In the next chapter, you will explore deeper conversations that enrich emotional intimacy and create a meaningful shared world.

Chapter 8
Deeper Conversations About Meaning and Identity

Most relationships begin with curiosity. In the early days, couples ask questions for hours. They share stories, hopes, fears, tiny memories and secret dreams. They listen closely because everything feels new.

> As time passes, partners still care deeply about each other, but life becomes busier. The days fill with responsibilities, routines, and tasks that must get done. Conversations shift from exploration to logistics.

You talk about schedules, groceries, chores, children and deadlines. You exchange information, but not meaning.

This shift is normal, but it creates silent drift. Without deeper conversations, partners may begin to feel like they know each other less than before. They may miss the emotional conversations that once brought them closer. They may feel connected on the surface but lonely underneath. The relationship becomes stable yet shallow, functional but less intimate.

Deep conversations are not dramatic or heavy. They are spacious. They create room for each partner's inner world. They help you discover who your partner is becoming and who you are becoming. They keep curiosity alive. They prevent the slow drift that happens when partners stop sharing the most important parts of themselves.

This chapter explores how to talk about meaning, identity, values, dreams, fears and change. These conversations create emotional intimacy that lasts. They help couples become not only partners in logistics but teammates in each other's lives. When you understand your partner's inner world, conflicts soften, empathy grows and closeness deepens.

Talking About Values, Dreams, Fears and Change

Many couples talk often, but they rarely talk deeply. Daily conversations tend to focus on what happened rather than what it meant. When partners do not explore values, fears and dreams, they begin to misunderstand each other without realizing it.

Deeper conversations help you stay connected across changing seasons of life. They bring clarity to questions like:

Who are you becoming.

What matters most to you now.

What feelings linger beneath the surface.

What do you hope for in the coming years.

What do you fear losing.

What do you want to build.

People change throughout life. Their desires shift. Their identity expands. Their values grow. If partners do not talk about these inner shifts, they risk waking up years later feeling like they have grown in different directions.

Here are the four types of deeper conversations that keep relationships aligned.

Conversations about values

Values are guiding principles. They shape choices, priorities and emotional reactions. When partners understand each other's values, many conflicts become easier to navigate because the couple can see the meaning behind the moment.

For example, one partner may value stability. The other may value freedom. These values influence decisions about money, schedules, work and lifestyle. Without conversation, the couple may argue about practical matters without understanding the deeper emotional foundation.

Talking about values helps partners understand each other with more empathy. These conversations can start with simple questions:

What matters most to you lately.

What value do you want to live more fully.

What experiences growing up shaped your values.

What makes you feel proud of who you are.

Values do not have to match perfectly. Couples thrive when they respect each other's values and find ways to support them.

Conversations about dreams

Dreams give life direction. They offer motivation, purpose and joy. Sharing dreams creates intimacy because it reveals vulnerability and longing. Many couples stop talking about dreams once life becomes busy, but dreams never stop evolving.

Dreams can be small, like learning a new skill. They can be large, like changing careers or building a life in a new place. They can be emotional, like wanting a calmer lifestyle or a deeper sense of creativity.

Talking about dreams helps partners support each other's growth. It also helps them imagine a shared future. A relationship becomes stronger when two people dream side by side.

Start with gentle questions:

What is one thing you are hoping for in the next year.

What is something you want to explore.

What is a dream you gave up that still lives inside you.

These conversations bring hope into the relationship.

Conversations about fears

Fears are tender places. They include fears of loss, fears of failure, fears of change or fears of not being enough. Many people hide fears because they worry it will burden their partner or make them appear weak. But sharing fears actually deepens trust. It shows vulnerability. It invites closeness.

When partners share fears, the relationship becomes a safe container where both people can be human. These conversations reduce misunderstanding because many emotional reactions come from hidden fears.

Questions that gently open fear conversations include:

What has been weighing on you recently.

Is there something you often worry about but rarely say.

When do you feel most insecure.

These conversations must be met with softness, patience and empathy.

Conversations about change

Change is constant. People grow, shift and evolve. Their needs change. Their goals change. Their emotional patterns change. When partners do not talk about change, outdated assumptions can quietly harm the relationship.

Talking about change keeps partners aligned. It helps them update their understanding of each other. It ensures that the relationship grows with both people rather than lagging behind.

Questions for exploring change include:

What has been shifting inside you lately.

What part of your life feels different now.

What are you learning about yourself.

These conversations help couples stay deeply connected through life's transitions.

How to Avoid Drifting Apart Quietly

Drift is subtle. It does not announce itself. It happens when partners gradually stop sharing their inner worlds. Drift is the slow erosion of curiosity. It is the quiet assumption that you already know everything about your partner. It is the belief that deeper conversations are not necessary.

Here are ways to prevent silent drift.

Stay curious about who your partner is becoming

Your partner is not the same person they were last year. They have changed in ways you may not see unless you ask. Curiosity keeps love alive. It also communicates respect. When partners feel genuinely seen, they stay emotionally connected.

You can say:

What is something new you have learned about yourself lately.

What has been inspiring you recently.

Curiosity is love in motion.

Create regular moments for deeper conversation

Do not wait for a perfect moment. Set aside small pockets of time for deeper talks. These can take place on a walk, at dinner, in the car or before bed. You do not need long hours. Even ten minutes can open emotional doors.

What matters is not the length of time but the quality of presence.

Share your inner world without waiting to be asked

Many partners wait for the other person to ask deeper questions. But deeper connection grows faster when both people volunteer their thoughts and feelings.

You might say:

Something I have been thinking about lately is…

Something that has been challenging for me is…

Sharing invites sharing.

Protect emotional space by reducing criticism during deeper talks

Nothing closes a partner faster than criticism or dismissal. During deeper conversations, focus on understanding rather than evaluating. The goal is emotional contact, not problem solving.

Offer validation, curiosity and warmth. These are the ingredients that keep conversations safe.

Revisit topics instead of treating them as one time disclosures

People reveal themselves slowly. A single conversation rarely uncovers the full picture. Revisiting meaningful topics keeps the connection fresh. It also shows your partner that you care about their inner world over time, not only in one moment.

Invite connection with gentle prompts

Many people want deeper conversations but do not know how to start them. Simple prompts create openings.

Examples:

What is something you want me to understand better about you.

What has been on your mind this week.

Small questions can lead to profound closeness.

Becoming Emotional Teammates

Becoming emotional teammates means supporting each other's inner lives. It means believing that your partner's feelings matter. It means approaching emotions with empathy rather than judgment. When partners become emotional teammates, the relationship becomes a refuge rather than a battlefield.

Here is what emotional teamwork looks like.

Listening with presence and without defensiveness

When your partner shares something vulnerable, the most supportive response is presence. You do not need solutions. You do not need perfect words. You simply need to listen with care.

Presence communicates, I am with you. I am on your side.

Acknowledging feelings even when you disagree with the content

Validation does not require agreement. You can acknowledge how something felt without agreeing with the interpretation.

For example:

I understand that felt painful.

I see how that affected you.

Validation creates emotional safety.

Encouraging each other's growth

Partners grow at different paces and in different directions. Emotional teammates support each other's development instead of fearing it.

You can ask:

What dream can I support right now.

What are you wanting to learn or explore.

Support creates shared pride and shared purpose.

Checking in regularly

Teammates communicate. Not only during crises, but consistently. Emotional teammates ask about hopes, pressures, insecurities and inspirations. They do not assume. They ask. They listen. They follow up.

Offering comfort without trying to take over

Comfort is gentle, not controlling. It comes through quiet presence, soft words, acts of support and emotional availability.

Examples:

I am here with you.

You do not have to go through this alone.

Comfort strengthens trust.

Sharing vulnerabilities openly

Emotional teammates reveal their fears, insecurities, joys and uncertainties. They do not hide behind perfection. They share honestly so their partner can understand them deeply.

Vulnerability builds intimacy. It also inspires vulnerability in return.

Celebrating each other's inner lives

Emotional teammates celebrate growth, not only achievements. They celebrate insights, self awareness, personal breakthroughs and emotional resilience.

Examples:

I love seeing you discover that part of yourself.

I am proud of how you handled that feeling.

These celebrations reinforce emotional connection.

Exercise: Twenty Questions for Deeper Bonding

Use these twenty questions to explore each other's inner worlds. Set aside time when both of you feel calm and open. You can take turns answering or choose a few questions at a time. The goal is curiosity, not speed.

1. What is one thing you are hoping for in the next year.

2. What has been on your mind lately that you have not shared.

3. What is something you want me to understand better about you.

4. What value feels most important to you right now.

5. What is something you are proud of that you rarely mention.

6. What has been inspiring you recently.

7. What fear has been quietly sitting in the background.

8. What dream feels alive for you right now.

9. What part of your identity has been changing.

10. What helps you feel emotionally safe with me.

11. What is something you miss that you would like to bring back into your life.

12. What is one stress that has been affecting you more than I may realize.

13. What is something you want us to create together.

14. What kind of support feels most nourishing to you these days.

15. What is something I do that helps you feel understood.

16. What is something I do that accidentally makes things harder.

17. What part of your life feels most meaningful right now.

18. What is something you are learning about yourself.

19. What brings you a sense of calm or comfort.

20. What are you excited about that you want to share with me.

These questions deepen intimacy because they reveal layers of experience, emotion and identity. Answer them slowly. Let each answer open the next door.

SCRIPTS FOR DEEPENING CONNECTION

Scripts for Deepening Connection

Script 1: Exploring dreams

What is one thing you are hoping for in the next year.

Script 2: Exploring identity

What is something you want me to understand better about you.

These scripts open the door to meaningful conversations.

Deeper conversations are the lifeblood of emotional intimacy. They keep your relationship alive, bright and connected. They remind you that love is not only shared routines but shared inner worlds. When partners talk about values, dreams, fears and change, they continue discovering each other year after year.

Avoiding drift is not about working harder. It is about staying curious. It is about not assuming you already know everything about your partner. It is about creating regular space where both of you can speak openly about who you are becoming.

When you become emotional teammates, you turn the relationship into a place where growth and vulnerability are welcomed. You build a foundation of trust that protects your connection through all life's changes.

In the next chapter, you will learn how to bring these deeper conversations into the realm of intimacy and desire, creating closeness on both emotional and physical levels.

Chapter 9
Intimacy and Desire Differences

Intimacy is one of the most meaningful parts of a relationship, yet it is also one of the hardest to talk about honestly. Many couples can discuss chores, plans, feelings and even conflicts with ease, but when the topic shifts to sexual connection, people often shut down. They become tense, embarrassed or quiet. They worry about saying the wrong thing or hurting their partner. They feel vulnerable and unsure. Yet few conversations have more power to strengthen or weaken a relationship.

> Sexual intimacy is not only about physical pleasure. It is about feeling safe, desired, seen and emotionally connected. It is about knowing that your partner accepts your body, your needs and your fears.

It is about trust. And like all forms of trust, intimacy grows with communication. When couples talk openly about intimacy, the relationship becomes more resilient. When they avoid these conversations, resentment and misunderstanding can quietly grow.

This chapter explores how to talk about sexual intimacy without shame, how to understand desire differences and how to build intimacy outside the bedroom that naturally supports closeness inside it. You will learn how to approach these conversations with kindness and curiosity, how to understand the emotional roots of desire and how to create a sexual connection that feels safe and satisfying for both partners.

Sex is not a separate category of the relationship. It is intertwined with emotional well being, communication habits, trust levels, daily connection and the overall climate of the partnership. When couples understand this, they stop treating sex as a performance and begin treating it as a form of emotional communication.

How to Talk About Sex Without Shame

Shame is one of the biggest barriers to healthy sexual communication. Many people grew up in environments where sex was discussed with secrecy, discomfort or judgment. Some absorbed messages that their desires were strange, that their bodies were flawed or that their sexuality should be silent. Others learned that sex was something to please a partner rather than something to explore together. These early messages linger and make conversations about intimacy feel dangerous or exposing.

Talking about sex requires vulnerability. It involves revealing desires, fears, insecurities and preferences. It involves trusting your partner to respond with care. When shame enters the conversation, people hide, minimize or dismiss their own needs. They avoid asking questions. They avoid telling the truth. They attempt to guess what the other person wants rather than communicating openly.

Here are ways to talk about sex with kindness and openness rather than shame.

Start gently and with emotional safety

Begin with the foundation. Before talking about physical intimacy, talk about emotional comfort and trust. Let your partner know that you want closeness, not confrontation. A simple sentence can ease tension.

Examples:

I want us to be able to talk about intimacy in a way that feels safe for both of us.

I care about our connection and I want us to explore this together.

These gentle openings help both partners relax.

Focus on curiosity instead of judgment

Approach intimacy with the same curiosity you bring to understanding your partner's emotions, dreams or values. Curiosity opens doors. Judgment closes them. You can ask:

What helps you feel connected before intimacy.

What makes intimacy enjoyable for you.

What helps you feel relaxed.

Curiosity invites honesty.

Use personal language rather than accusatory language

Instead of saying, You never initiate, say, I sometimes wonder what goes through your mind when it comes to initiating.

Instead of, You do not care about sex, say, I miss feeling close physically and I want to understand how you feel about it.

Personal language reduces defensiveness and keeps the conversation warm.

Share your inner world with kindness

Being honest about your desires or insecurities is not selfish. It is essential. You might say:

Here is what feels good emotionally and physically for me.

Here is something that helps me feel close.

Here is something that makes me feel anxious or insecure.

Honesty builds intimacy far more than quiet accommodation.

Move slowly and check in often

Sexual conversations can stir emotions. Go slowly. Ask for feedback.

Is this conversation feeling okay for you.

Do you want to pause.

Should we come back to this later.

The goal is not to rush. The goal is to stay connected while talking.

Avoid comparisons

Comparing your partner to past partners, to other couples or to imagined ideals damages trust. Intimacy is unique to the two of you. Its purpose is connection, not measurement.

Normalize desire differences

Desire differences are common. They do not mean one partner is flawed. They simply mean the couple needs understanding, not shame. You will learn more about this later in the chapter.

When partners talk about sex without shame, intimacy becomes a place of freedom rather than pressure.

Understanding Desire Mismatches

One of the most common sources of tension in long term relationships is desire mismatch. These mismatches occur when partners differ in how often they want sexual intimacy, how they feel desire, how quickly they become aroused, what helps them feel ready for sex, or how emotional and physical intimacy connect for them. These differences are normal. They happen in every relationship.

Desire mismatches become painful not because the desires differ, but because the partners misunderstand the meaning behind those differences. One partner might interpret lower desire as rejection. The other might interpret higher desire as pressure. Both might misread each other's intentions.

Understanding desire means understanding the emotional and physiological patterns that shape it. Here are some insights that help couples navigate desire differences with compassion.

Desire is influenced by stress, fatigue and emotional climate

Desire is not simply a physical impulse. It is shaped by the nervous system. When people are tired, stressed, overwhelmed, anxious or emotionally distant, desire often decreases. The partner with lower desire is not rejecting the other. Their body is signaling a need for regulation.

When couples understand this, they stop taking desire differences personally. They begin to look at the broader emotional environment rather than blaming themselves or each other.

Desire develops differently for different people

Some people experience desire spontaneously. They feel interest first, then seek connection.

Others experience desire responsively. They do not feel

spontaneous desire but become aroused when they feel emotionally safe, relaxed or physically stimulated.

Neither style is wrong. They are simply different. Conflict arises when partners expect each other to feel desire in the same way.

Understanding your pattern and your partner's pattern reduces frustration and increases compassion.

Emotional intimacy is the doorway to physical intimacy for many people

For many individuals, desire grows from emotional closeness. When they feel understood, appreciated, connected and safe, desire naturally increases. When emotional distance grows, desire fades.

This does not mean their desire is conditional. It means intimacy is a whole body and whole heart experience.

Initiation styles often differ

One partner may initiate directly. The other may initiate subtly through gestures, touch or closeness. When partners misinterpret each other's initiation style, they may feel ignored or rejected. Understanding each other's style prevents miscommunication.

Desire differences can be balanced with communication

Couples rarely settle desire differences through compromise alone. They settle them through understanding. When both partners feel heard and respected, intimacy becomes easier to navigate. When partners share what helps them feel ready for intimacy, desire becomes easier to spark.

You might ask each other:

What helps you feel open to intimacy.

What makes it harder for you.

What helps you feel wanted.

What shuts you down.

These questions create a map of each partner's inner world.

Creating Intimacy Outside the Bedroom That Supports Intimacy Inside It

Sexual intimacy does not begin in the bedroom. It begins in daily life. It begins when partners treat each other with kindness, curiosity and appreciation. It begins when the emotional climate feels safe. It begins when couples feel like teammates.

Here are ways to build intimacy outside the bedroom that naturally strengthens physical closeness.

Build emotional safety

Emotional safety is the foundation of sexual safety. When partners feel secure, their bodies relax. Stress decreases. Desire becomes more accessible. Emotional safety comes from gentle tones, reliable communication and showing care in difficult moments.

Without emotional safety, physical intimacy can feel pressured or out of reach.

Practice daily affection without sexual expectation

Affection builds closeness, but affection that always leads to sex can feel pressuring. Use affection to communicate warmth rather than obligation.

Examples:

a soft touch

a hug

holding hands

a gentle kiss

a warm smile

When affection is not tied to immediate sexual activity, partners feel more relaxed and open.

Share emotional intimacy regularly

When partners share thoughts, feelings, hopes and fears, the bond strengthens. Emotional intimacy is fuel for physical intimacy. It keeps the relationship alive.

Asking deeper questions, being curious about each other and sharing personal reflections all support sexual closeness.

Cultivate playful connection

Playfulness builds chemistry. Flirting, humor, teasing in a kind way and creating inside jokes strengthen emotional connection. When partners feel playful, intimacy becomes lighter rather than pressured.

Play signals safety. Safety opens desire.

Create moments of presence

Presence is one of the most powerful forms of intimacy. Presence means slowing down enough to truly see your partner. It might include sharing a quiet moment with no devices, taking a walk, cooking together or simply sitting without distraction.

Presence fosters closeness, and closeness fosters desire.

Reduce emotional friction in daily life

Small irritations, unresolved conflicts and communication habits can impact sexual desire. When daily life feels full of tension, intimacy becomes harder. Working on communication, expressing appreciation, resolving conflicts and practicing kindness make the bedroom feel like a place of connection rather than a place of pressure.

Express what feels good emotionally and physically

Your partner cannot read your mind. Sharing what helps you feel emotionally connected is just as important as sharing what feels physically pleasurable.

A script that helps is:

Here is what feels good emotionally and physically for me.

This opens the door to mutual learning and exploration.

Move at a pace that feels comfortable for both partners

Sexual intimacy should be an invitation, not an expectation. You can say:

Can we explore this together at a pace that feels comfortable for both of us.

This phrase creates connection, not pressure.

How to Have Hard Conversations About Sex

Talking about intimacy can stir fear and vulnerability, especially when discussing desire differences or frustrations. Here is how to have these conversations in a loving way.

• • •

Speak with kindness and clarity

You can communicate needs without criticism. Try to describe your feelings rather than evaluating your partner.

Examples:

I miss feeling close physically.

I want us to explore intimacy with curiosity.

I feel nervous talking about this, but I want us to understand each other.

Kindness makes hard conversations softer.

Listen without defensiveness

When your partner talks about intimacy, they are sharing something vulnerable. Try to hear the feeling behind their words rather than focusing on the details. Validation matters more than solutions.

Avoid blame and shame

Statements like You do not care about sex or You never want intimacy create emotional shutdown. Instead, express your experience.

Examples:

I sometimes feel unsure about how to connect physically.

I sometimes wonder what helps you feel desire.

This keeps the conversation open rather than reactive.

Find shared goals

Instead of seeing desire differences as problems, view them as opportunities to grow together. Create goals that honor both partners.

Examples:

Let us explore intimacy that feels good for both of us.

Let us talk openly about what we enjoy.

Shared goals create teamwork.

Exercise: Yes, No, Maybe Intimacy List for Couples

This exercise helps couples talk about intimacy in a structured and comfortable way. It encourages exploration without pressure.

Step 1: Each partner makes three lists.

Yes list:

Activities or forms of intimacy you enjoy or want to explore.

No list:

Activities or forms of intimacy that do not feel right or comfortable.

Maybe list:

Possibilities you are unsure about or open to exploring with conversation and care.

Include emotional and physical items. For example:

Yes list examples:

gentle touch

cuddling

more time for kissing

slow build up

sharing fantasies softly

talking during intimacy

No list examples:

certain positions

interactions that trigger insecurity

anything that feels pressured

Maybe list examples:

trying new forms of touch

using music or lighting

different pacing

Step 2: Share your lists with curiosity.

Take turns. Listen to each other. Ask questions gently. Validate feelings.

Step 3: Choose one or two items from the yes list to explore together.

Small steps build trust.

Step 4: Revisit the lists every few months.

Desires evolve. Comfort grows with communication.

This exercise reduces guessing and creates shared understanding.

SCRIPTS FOR INTIMACY CONVERSATIONS

Script 1: Emotional and physical clarity

Here is what feels good emotionally and physically for me.

Script 2: Exploring intimacy at a comfortable pace

Can we explore this together at a pace that feels comfortable for both of us.

These scripts help partners speak honestly without pressure.

Sexual intimacy is a living part of the relationship. It breathes, shifts and evolves over time. It reflects emotional closeness, relational health and the patterns partners bring into the relationship. When couples talk about intimacy openly, they strengthen trust and reduce shame. When they understand desire differences with compassion, they stop taking things personally. When they nurture intimacy outside the bedroom, their physical connection naturally deepens.

Intimacy is not a separate world. It is woven into the routines, emotions, tone and habits of daily life. It grows where there is curiosity, safety, kindness and honest communication. When couples become teammates in intimacy, they create a space of pleasure, exploration and connection that enriches the relationship in every dimension.

Part 4

The Hard Talks Every Couple Eventually Faces

Chapter 10
Money: One of the Biggest Communication Stressors

Money is one of the most emotionally charged topics in any relationship. It affects daily life, future plans, personal identity, feelings of security and a couple's sense of teamwork. Yet money is also one of the hardest things to talk about calmly. Even couples who communicate well about feelings, sex, conflict or parenting often struggle when the conversation shifts to finances. Money feels different. It feels personal, raw and revealing. It brings up fears and expectations that many people never fully understood until they attempted to manage money with a partner.

> Money conversations create stress because they carry emotional weight far beyond numbers. When partners talk about spending, saving or debt, they are not only talking about money. They are talking about safety, trust, identity, control, independence, childhood history, dreams and fear of the future.

These layers create tension. One partner may fear not having enough. The other may fear being controlled. One may see money as a tool for enjoyment. The other may see it as an anchor for security. Without deeper understanding, financial conversations can easily become arguments.

The good news is that couples can learn to have calm, compassionate and productive money conversations. You do not need to become financial experts. You only need emotional clarity, shared values and simple communication habits that help both partners feel heard and respected. Money becomes less frightening when both people understand the emotional stories behind each other's patterns.

This chapter explores why money conversations feel personal, how to discuss financial choices without conflict, how to uncover hidden expectations and how financial transparency builds trust. You will learn how to talk about money in a way that strengthens partnership instead of weakening it. You will also find a worksheet that helps you discover your personal money story and scripts that help you speak clearly without shame.

Money is not just about math. It is about meaning.

Why Money Talks Feel Personal

Money is woven into every part of life. It touches personal history, cultural messages, self worth, survival instincts and unspoken fears. This is why financial conversations often feel more emotional than practical.

Here are the main reasons why money talks feel personal and often trigger strong reactions.

Money shapes our sense of security

Every person has an internal scale of what feels safe financially. For some, security means having a stable income. For others, it means having savings, low debt or clear plans. When financial decisions feel uncertain or unpredictable, the nervous system reacts. The body interprets financial insecurity as real danger. Arguments start not because someone is wrong, but because someone is scared.

Money reflects personal identity

People often attach identity to financial habits. Being frugal may feel tied to being responsible. Being generous may feel tied to being kind. Enjoying luxuries may feel tied to a sense of freedom. When financial choices differ, partners may interpret those differences as personal judgments rather than practical disagreements.

A partner who saves may feel proud of their discipline. A partner who spends on experiences may feel proud of their ability to live fully. When these identities collide, misunderstandings appear.

Money carries childhood memories

Every person grows up with a financial atmosphere that shapes their beliefs. Some grew up in scarcity and learned to fear running out. Some grew up in comfort and never thought about money. Some grew up with stress around bills and absorbed worry. Some grew up watching parents fight about money, making financial conversations feel threatening even decades later.

When money talks trigger emotional reactions, those reactions often come from old memories rather than the current situation.

Money relates to power and independence

Money influences decisions, autonomy and lifestyle. For some people, managing money well feels like personal freedom. For others, sharing money feels vulnerable. Couples sometimes argue about finances when the real conflict is about independence, control or fairness.

Without naming these deeper feelings, money talks easily become personal battles.

Money reflects hidden expectations about partnership

Many people enter relationships assuming their partner shares their financial values. They expect agreement on saving, spending, vacations, generosity, gifts and long term financial goals. When these expectations are unspoken, disappointment follows.

Money disagreements are often expectation disagreements.

· · ·

Money affects the future

Financial choices shape long term plans. They influence careers, family decisions, housing, lifestyle and retirement. When partners disagree about financial direction, it can feel like disagreeing about the future of the relationship itself.

These layers make money talks understandably personal and emotional. When couples understand the emotional roots of their reactions, they can approach money conversations with much more patience and compassion.

How to Discuss Spending, Saving and Stress Calmly

Calm money conversations do not happen automatically. They happen when partners create structure, soften their tone and approach finances as a team rather than as opponents. Here are tools that help couples discuss finances without triggering arguments or shame.

Set aside a specific time for money talks

Money conversations often go poorly when they happen in the middle of stress or exhaustion. They also go poorly when one partner is surprised by the topic. Plan financial conversations the way you plan important meetings. Choose a calm moment. Sit together. Approach it with willingness rather than urgency.

This simple habit removes pressure and increases emotional safety.

• • •

Start with emotional grounding, not numbers

Before discussing expenses, budgets or goals, begin with statements that reduce tension and affirm partnership.

Examples:

I want us to feel secure together.

We are on the same team.

Let us talk about this in a way that keeps us connected.

These grounding statements remind both partners that the goal is not winning a debate. The goal is building a shared life.

Share the emotional meaning behind your habits

Behind every financial habit is an emotional story. Without understanding these stories, partners make inaccurate assumptions about each other.

Use this script to begin sharing:

Here is what money meant in my family and how it still affects me.

For example:

One person may say, In my family, money was unpredictable. We never knew if bills would be paid. So now I save aggressively because uncertainty scares me.

The other may say, In my family, money was used to create joy. We spent freely on experiences. So I tend to focus on enjoyment rather than saving.

These stories transform judgment into understanding.

Use gentle language to express concerns

Instead of accusatory statements like, You always overspend, try:

I feel anxious when I see expenses rise because financial insecurity is a fear I carry.

or

I feel stressed when we avoid financial planning because I want to feel prepared.

Gentle language keeps the conversation open.

Focus on needs and goals instead of blame

Money conversations improve when partners identify shared goals:

security

travel

a home

reduced debt

freedom to change careers

supporting family

creating experiences

When the conversation becomes about shared goals, the couple becomes a team.

You can say:

Let us plan this together so both of us feel secure.

Shared goals reduce defensiveness and increase cooperation.

Create rules for money conversations

Couples often find these rules helpful:

No interrupting.

No raising voices.

No bringing up past financial mistakes.

No shaming language.

Pause if emotions rise.

Return to connection before returning to numbers.

Rules create the emotional safety needed for productive conversation.

Separate financial facts from emotional reactions

Facts might include income, expenses or savings. Emotional reactions might include fear, anger, shame or guilt.

When partners name the emotion separately from the number, communication becomes much clearer.

For example:

The fact is that we spent more this month.

My emotional reaction is fear because I do not want us to fall behind.

This clarity prevents spiraling arguments.

Collaborate on financial roles

Some couples naturally divide financial tasks. One partner may enjoy budgeting. The other may enjoy long term planning. The problem arises when partnership turns into control.

Discuss roles openly:

Who manages bills.

Who monitors accounts.

Who tracks goals.

How often do we review together.

Roles must feel fair and transparent. No partner should feel shut out or overwhelmed.

Create calm systems instead of relying on memory

Budgets, savings plans and automatic transfers reduce stress because they remove guesswork. When systems are clear, arguments decrease.

· · ·

Celebrate progress

Money conversations often focus on problems, but celebrating progress increases motivation and connection.

Examples:

We paid off a credit card.

We saved consistently this month.

We communicated well.

We managed a stressful conversation calmly.

Celebration reinforces teamwork.

Hidden Expectations and Financial Transparency

Behind every money argument is at least one hidden expectation. Partners rarely realize they carry these expectations until they collide. Financial transparency helps bring these expectations into the open and prevents misunderstandings.

Here are the most common hidden expectations couples struggle with.

Expectations about spending priorities

One partner may expect to spend freely on experiences. Another may prioritize saving. Without discussion, these assumptions clash.

Ask each other:

What matters most to you when you think about spending.

What purchases feel meaningful.

What purchases feel stressful.

These conversations clarify values.

Expectations about saving and security

What feels safe to one partner may feel restrictive to another. Saving can symbolize responsibility for one and scarcity for another.

Discuss:

How much savings helps you feel secure.

How much flexibility feels necessary.

Security varies by person. Understanding this reduces conflict.

Expectations about lifestyle

Lifestyle expectations often come from childhood. One partner may expect vacations every year. The other may expect modest living. These assumptions feel natural until partners realize they differ.

Expectations about financial roles

Hidden expectations may include:

One person should handle budgeting.

One person should earn more.

Both partners should contribute equally.

The higher earner should make more decisions.

The partner who stays home should not spend freely.

These expectations can create resentment if never discussed.

Expectations about generosity and gifts

Partners may disagree about:

how much to spend on celebrations

how much to give to family

whether surprises or luxuries are important

These expectations reflect emotional values.

Expectations around debt

Debt brings emotional weight. Some see debt as a normal part of life. Others see it as a burden. Talking openly about comfort levels with debt prevents fear driven conflict.

Expectations about independence

Money can create discomfort when independence interacts with partnership. One partner may value freedom to spend within reason. The other may value joint planning for everything.

Nothing creates conflict faster than assuming your partner sees money the same way you do.

Financial Transparency Builds Trust

Transparency means clarity about financial realities, choices and concerns. It is not about sharing every transaction in detail unless that is what the couple agrees on. It is about fairness, honesty and partnership.

Transparency builds trust in several ways:

It removes fear of financial secrets.

It prevents accidental surprises.

It reduces assumptions.

It ensures that both partners feel involved.

It strengthens teamwork.

Transparency includes:

sharing income

sharing debts

sharing financial goals

sharing concerns

reviewing accounts periodically

When partners are transparent, the relationship feels fair and stable.

Exercise: Money Stories Worksheet

Use this exercise to understand your personal money story and share it with your partner. Complete it separately and then discuss together.

Part 1: Childhood money atmosphere

Describe the atmosphere around money in your childhood.

Examples: calm, stressed, unpredictable, abundant, scarce, secretive.

Part 2: Key memories

Write down two or three memories that shaped your beliefs about money.

Examples: parents fighting about bills, being told not to waste money, moments of generosity.

Part 3: Core emotions

Identify emotions you feel when thinking about money today.

fear

control

freedom

anxiety

shame

security

pride

Part 4: Adult financial habits

Describe your typical habits.

Do you save quickly.

Spend impulsively.

Avoid checking accounts.

Over research purchases.

Part 5: Triggers

Identify what triggers financial stress for you.

unexpected expenses

debt

large purchases

lack of planning

feeling controlled

Part 6: Personal financial values

What values guide your decisions.

security

comfort

freedom

minimalism

growth

generosity

Part 7: Share with your partner

Use this script to begin:

Here is what money meant in my family and how it still affects me.

Take turns listening and validating. Avoid judgment.

SCRIPTS FOR MONEY CONVERSATIONS

Script 1: Sharing money history

Here is what money meant in my family and how it still affects me.

Script 2: Planning with partnership

Let us plan this together so both of us feel secure.

Use these scripts whenever money feels tense. They shift the conversation from fear to teamwork.

Money does not have to divide couples. It can become a place of deeper understanding, shared purpose and emotional growth. When partners talk openly about their money stories, they understand not only financial habits but emotional histories. When they approach money as teammates, stress decreases. When expectations become clear, trust increases. When transparency becomes standard, the relationship feels safer.

Money is not only about numbers. It is about meaning. It is about emotion. It is about patterns learned long ago. It is about dreams for the future. It is about security and freedom and identity. When couples approach money with curiosity, patience and honesty, financial conversations become opportunities for connection rather than conflict.

Your financial life is not separate from your emotional life. It is part of your partnership. When you learn to navigate money together, you strengthen the relationship in ways that extend far beyond bank accounts.

Chapter 11
Trust, Mistakes and Repairing After Hurt

Trust is the quiet foundation of a relationship. It is not built in a single moment, nor is it maintained with grand gestures. It grows slowly through consistent actions, honest communication and emotional reliability. When trust is strong, the relationship feels like a safe home. When trust is shaken, everything inside the relationship trembles. Conversations become tense. Assumptions become heavier. Small moments feel uncertain. Emotional safety changes shape.

> Every couple faces moments when trust cracks. Sometimes these cracks are small, such as white lies or emotional withdrawal.
> Sometimes they are larger, such as secrecy, hidden habits, financial dishonesty or betrayals that shake the relationship deeply.

Many couples feel ashamed or hopeless when trust erodes, but trust is not an all or nothing state. It is not permanent damage. Trust can be rebuilt with patience, honesty and consistent effort. In many cases, the process of repair creates a stronger bond than before because the couple learns to communicate more openly and honestly than they ever knew how to before.

This chapter explores how to talk about lies, secrecy and betrayals, both small and large. It explains what genuine repair looks like and how trust can be rebuilt slowly and honestly. You will learn how to approach painful conversations without causing more harm, how to express accountability in a way that heals rather than wounds, and how to create a repair process that feels real and sustainable.

Mistakes do not destroy relationships. Avoidance does. Silence does. Pretending nothing happened does. What heals relationships is willingness, truth, humility and effort.

How to Talk About Lies, Secrecy and Betrayals

Talking about hurt is painful. It triggers fear, shame, defensiveness, sadness and anger. Many people avoid these conversations because they worry it will make things worse. Others minimize what happened because they feel ashamed. But pain cannot heal in silence. It can only heal in truth.

To repair trust, the couple needs a structure for talking about hurt in a way that is safe enough for both partners. This requires patience, gentleness and clarity. Here are the principles that make difficult conversations more healing and less damaging.

Create emotional safety before beginning

Trust conversations should not happen in the middle of an argument or when one partner feels overwhelmed. Choose a calm moment. Begin with a grounding intention:

I want us to talk about this in a way that keeps us connected.

I want to understand and repair this together.

This intention does not erase the hurt, but it makes the conversation safe enough for honesty.

Speak the truth without hiding and without dramatizing

Honesty must be clear and steady. You can use the script:

I want to be fully honest about what happened and why.

This does not mean unloading every detail if the detail is unnecessary and harmful. It means providing truthful information that restores clarity and helps your partner understand reality. Avoid minimizing and avoid exaggerating. Stay grounded in facts and feelings.

Avoid defensive explanations

Explaining the reasons behind a mistake can be helpful, but only after full accountability is expressed. Defensiveness shifts focus to self protection instead of healing. Accountability requires saying:

Here is what I did.

Here is how I imagine it hurt you.

Here is why I think I made that choice.

Accountability must precede explanation.

Allow room for emotion without taking it as punishment

Your partner may feel angry, sad, confused or afraid. These emotions are natural responses to hurt. They are not punishments. They are not attacks. They are feelings.

If you are the one who broke trust, your responsibility is to stay present and listen to the emotions without defending yourself. You do not need to fix the feelings. You only need to witness them with care.

Ask what your partner needs in order to feel understood

Understanding is the first step in repair. You can ask:

What do you need to feel heard right now.

What part of this still feels unclear.

What hurts the most for you.

These questions create emotional closeness even in painful moments.

Name the hurt with tenderness

Name the emotional impact of the moment with compassion.

I see that this hurt you deeply.

I understand that my choices made you feel unsafe.

I see how this shook your trust.

Naming hurt does not weaken you. It strengthens repair.

Avoid blame shifting

Statements like You made me feel unappreciated so I lied or I would not have done this if you did not act that way create more damage and prevent healing. Mistakes can have context, but context should never shift responsibility onto the injured partner.

Stay on the same team

Even in difficult conversations, frame the process as collaborative. The couple is facing the problem together, not fighting against each other.

You can say:

I want us to move through this together.

I want us to find a way forward that feels healing for both of us.

The tone of teamwork creates safety.

Types of Trust Breaks and Their Emotional Roots

Not all betrayals look the same. Some are small yet repeated. Some are large and shocking. Some are emotional rather than physical. Each type of trust break requires understanding and intention.

Here are common categories of trust rupture in relationships.

Lies of convenience

These include small lies meant to avoid conflict. Examples include hiding a spending choice, lying about finishing a task or concealing small mistakes. While they may seem minor, repeated small lies erode trust slowly.

Lies of omission

These involve withholding information because the partner fears judgment or discomfort. Omission can create a sense of distance because it prevents authentic connection.

Secrecy around habits or behaviors

This includes hiding financial habits, online interactions, personal struggles, addictions or emotional connections. Secrecy creates emotional walls and leads the other partner to question what else is unseen.

Emotional betrayals

These include forming a close connection with someone outside the relationship that crosses emotional boundaries.

Emotional betrayals often feel just as painful as physical betrayals because they involve intimacy and attention.

Physical betrayals

Physical affairs or intimate conduct with someone else create deep wounds. These betrayals require intensive honesty, emotional patience and long term rebuilding.

Betrayals of reliability

Failing to show up when promised, breaking repeated agreements or not following through on important commitments also break trust. Reliability is a core form of safety.

Betrayals of secrecy in communication

Sharing private information with others or discussing sensitive issues with external people instead of your partner can weaken trust.

Understanding the nature of the rupture helps partners create an appropriate repair plan.

What Genuine Repair Looks Like

Repair is not a single apology or a dramatic statement. It is a process. It unfolds over time. Genuine repair is built on consistency, honesty and empathy. It recognizes that healing happens slowly. For trust to rebuild, both partners need clarity about what real repair involves.

Here are the elements of genuine repair.

Full and honest acknowledgment

The injured partner needs clarity. They need to understand what happened, why it happened and how long it happened for. Repair begins when the partner who caused harm acknowledges the truth completely and calmly.

Examples:

I understand what I did and I understand why it hurt you.

I take responsibility for my actions without excuse.

Acknowledgment turns chaos into clarity.

Empathy for the emotional impact

The injured partner needs to know that their emotions make sense. Empathy is not simply saying, I am sorry you feel that way. It is saying:

I see how this broke your trust.

I see why this makes you afraid.

I understand the depth of your pain.

Empathy repairs emotional connection.

. . .

A willingness to answer questions

The injured partner often needs information in order to feel grounded. Their mind will create worst case scenarios unless given clarity. The partner rebuilding trust needs to answer questions with patience. Some questions may be painful, but they are part of rebuilding.

Openness to discomfort

Repair is uncomfortable for both partners. The one who broke trust feels shame or guilt. The one who was hurt feels fear or anger. Real repair requires staying present through discomfort rather than shutting down or withdrawing.

Patience with the healing process

Trust does not return quickly. Even after sincere repair, waves of insecurity can return. These emotional waves are normal. The partner who caused hurt must respond with patience rather than frustration.

Examples:

I understand you are feeling insecure again.

I am here and I want to support your healing.

Patience builds long term trust.

Clear and consistent behavior change

Apologies without changed behavior do not rebuild trust. Actions must demonstrate reliability, transparency and commitment. The partner must show, not only say, that they are rebuilding trust.

Behavior change might include:

increased transparency

new communication habits

seeking support or therapy

setting boundaries

removing triggers of secrecy

Consistency is more important than perfection.

Rebuilding emotional closeness slowly

Trust repair involves emotional reconnection. This includes conversations about fears, needs and hopes. The couple rebuilds through shared vulnerability, not rushed forgiveness.

Invitations for the hurt partner to share needs

The injured partner needs space to voice what would help them feel more secure. These requests must be reasonable, but they are essential.

Examples:

I need more transparency for a while.

I need reassurance when I feel insecure.

I need you to check in with me when something triggers fear.

These needs guide the healing process.

A shared commitment to the future

Repair succeeds when both partners want to rebuild. They create a shared vision for trust. They talk about what they want to protect, what they want to learn and what kind of relationship they hope to build together.

How to Rebuild Trust Slowly and Honestly

Trust is rebuilt through small moments, not grand promises. It returns through predictability, care, honesty and consistency. Here is how couples can rebuild trust slowly and sustainably.

Transparency increases emotional safety

Transparency does not mean policing each other. It means clarity about behaviors that matter. Transparency helps the injured partner feel grounded rather than trapped in uncertainty.

Examples include:

sharing schedules

checking in when plans change

opening communication about emotional struggles

providing clarity when triggers appear

Transparency is not control. It is reassurance.

Daily reliability matters more than dramatic statements

When trust is broken, the injured partner watches for consistency. They look for patterns that show stability. Small acts of reliability matter more than emotional speeches.

Reliability looks like:

keeping promises

being where you said you would be

following through on commitments

being emotionally available

checking in regularly

These habits rebuild trust quietly.

Emotional reassurance supports healing

The hurt partner may fear instability, abandonment or repeated betrayal. Reassurance softens these fears.

Examples:

I am here and committed to repairing this.

Your feelings make sense.

We are working through this together.

Reassurance must be repeated often.

Avoiding secrecy becomes part of the new relationship culture

Secrecy erodes trust quickly. During repair, couples often choose a period of increased openness. This might include sharing conversations, schedules or certain online interactions until stability returns.

Rebuilding intimacy when both feel ready

After hurt, intimacy can feel complicated. Emotional closeness must be restored before physical closeness can feel safe. Couples rebuild intimacy slowly through honesty, vulnerability and consistent connection.

Examples:

gentle affection

open conversations

shared experiences

small acts of care

Intimacy returns through emotional safety.

Addressing root causes

Repair also means understanding what made the betrayal

possible. This does not excuse the behavior. It helps prevent it from happening again. Root causes might include:

stress

avoidance

fear of conflict

emotional distance

personal insecurities

lack of skill in communication

Examining root causes helps the couple grow.

Setting boundaries that support healing

Boundaries protect the relationship. They might involve:

limiting contact with certain people

reducing privacy in specific areas for a period of time

agreeing on communication guidelines

checking in when triggers arise

Boundaries must be mutual and respectful.

Seeking support when needed

Sometimes couples need external help to navigate trust repair. Therapy, coaching or a trusted mentor can help both partners manage emotions and rebuild communication.

Seeking support is not failure. It is commitment.

Celebrating progress

Healing is slow, but progress deserves recognition. Celebrate moments of closeness, honest conversations and consistent trust building. Progress strengthens hope.

Exercise: Guided Repair Conversation Template

Use this template during a calm moment. Sit together and move through each step slowly. The goal is connection, clarity and emotional safety.

Step 1: Opening intention

Both partners state a calm intention.

Examples:

I want to understand and rebuild trust together.

I want to repair this in a way that strengthens us.

Step 2: Honest description

The partner who broke trust speaks clearly, using the script:

I want to be fully honest about what happened and why.

Avoid minimizing or dramatizing. Speak gently and truthfully.

Step 3: Acknowledgment of impact

The partner who caused hurt says:

I see how this impacted you. I see how this hurt your trust.

The injured partner shares their feelings, knowing they are safe to express them.

Step 4: Clarifying questions

The hurt partner may ask questions that help them understand. The partner answering stays patient and grounded.

Step 5: Emotional needs

The hurt partner shares what they need to feel safer.

Examples:

I need more openness for a while.

I need reassurance when I feel insecure.

Step 6: Commitment to change

The partner rebuilding trust says:

Here is what I am willing to do to rebuild trust.

List commitments clearly and realistically.

Step 7: Closing

End with a gentle statement of connection.

Examples:

We are working through this together.

I appreciate your willingness to repair this.

This guided conversation builds structure and safety around a tender topic.

SCRIPTS FOR TRUST REPAIR

Script 1: Complete honesty

I want to be fully honest about what happened and why.

Script 2: Commitment to rebuilding

Here is what I am willing to do to rebuild trust.

Use these scripts to anchor difficult conversations in clarity and care.

Every relationship faces hurt. Every relationship experiences ruptures in trust, whether small or large. These moments do not define the future unless the couple refuses to face them. What defines a relationship is how partners respond to hurt. Some couples pull away. Others lean in. Those who choose honesty, patience and consistent repair often build deeper closeness than before the rupture.

Trust is rebuilt slowly. It returns through presence, through truth, through patterns of reliability. It returns when partners stay kind even when they feel vulnerable. It returns when both people choose the relationship again and again, even during discomfort.

When couples learn how to talk about lies, secrecy and betrayal with compassion, they build emotional strength. When they understand what genuine repair requires, they become more resilient. When they rebuild trust honestly, they create a relationship grounded in transparency and mutual care.

This chapter is not about perfection. It is about courage. The courage to speak truth. The courage to face pain. The courage to rebuild something meaningful.

In the next chapter, you will explore how life transitions, stress and changing roles can affect a relationship and how to stay connected through seasons of uncertainty and growth.

Chapter 12
Technology, Distraction and Presence

Technology is woven into nearly every part of modern life. Phones wake us up. Notifications guide our schedules. Messages, emails and alerts fill our days. Social media presents endless streams of information that can feel urgent even when it is not. Technology brings convenience, connection and entertainment, but it also brings distraction. It pulls attention away from the people who matter most, often without us realizing it. What begins as a quick glance at a screen can easily turn into minutes or hours of emotional distance.

> Many couples today face a challenge that earlier generations never had to navigate. They share a home but not always presence. They sit together on the couch yet live in separate digital worlds.

They eat meals side by side yet engage more with their phones than with each other. Not because they do not care, but because technology is designed to capture attention. When attention is captured, presence fades. When presence fades, closeness weakens.

This chapter explores the emotional impact of technology on relationships. It looks at how phones, social media and digital habits create subtle forms of disconnection. It helps couples recognize the difference between sharing physical space and sharing emotional presence. You will learn how to talk about tech without blame, how to create boundaries that support intimacy and how to protect your connection while living in a digital world.

Technology is not the enemy. Disconnection is. When partners learn how to balance digital life with relationship needs, technology becomes a tool rather than a barrier.

Phones, Social Media, Emotional Affairs and Drifting Apart

Most couples do not argue about phones because of screen time itself. They argue because of what the phone represents in emotional terms. A phone that pulls attention away communicates disinterest. A partner absorbed in social media may unintentionally signal that digital connection is more important than the relationship. When this happens often, the other partner begins to feel invisible. This creates early stages of drift.

Drifting apart rarely begins with a dramatic event. It begins in these quiet moments of divided attention. It begins with evenings where partners sit together physically but not emotionally. It begins with conversations interrupted by notifications. It begins when one partner feels unheard because the other is multitasking. It begins when the digital world competes with the relationship and often wins.

Here are common ways technology affects intimacy.

Constant phone checking reduces emotional presence

A relationship needs focused attention to thrive. Even small interruptions interrupt emotional flow. When a partner checks a phone mid conversation, the message received is often, Something else matters more than this moment. Even if that is not the intention, the emotional impact is real.

Presence is a form of love. Distraction feels like its opposite.

Social media creates comparison and insecurity

Social media often shows curated lives that appear happier, wealthier, more romantic or more stable than reality. This can trigger insecurity, envy or dissatisfaction. Couples may compare their connection to unrealistic images. They may feel pressure to perform rather than connect.

Insecurity can also grow when partners interact with others online in ways that feel ambiguous. Likes, comments, inside jokes or private messages can become emotional stumbling blocks if they are not communicated openly.

Digital conversations can become emotional replacements

Sometimes people turn to digital interactions for emotional fulfillment, especially when they feel lonely or disconnected at home. What begins as a casual conversation with a coworker or online friend can grow into an emotional bond that crosses boundaries. Emotional affairs often begin with texting, messaging or sharing personal information.

These connections feel safe, private and instantly rewarding. They do not require the vulnerability or accountability of real world intimacy. But they drain emotional energy away from the relationship and create secrecy, which weakens trust.

Emotional affairs hurt because they redirect intimacy. They make a partner feel replaced long before any physical betrayal occurs.

Multitasking during meaningful moments creates emotional gaps

Trying to listen to a partner while scrolling a phone does not create genuine connection. Multitasking divides attention, and divided attention sends the message that the relationship is not valued. Partners may begin to withdraw emotionally when they feel they are competing with a device.

Technology becomes an escape from unresolved tension

When conflict feels overwhelming, a partner may retreat into digital life to avoid discomfort. They may scroll, watch videos or immerse themselves in entertainment. This avoidance can create emotional distance that grows larger over time.

Avoidance is understandable, but if it replaces repair and communication, the relationship suffers.

Devices disrupt rituals of closeness

Many couples lose important bonding rituals because of technology. Such rituals include talking in bed, eating meals together, winding down at night or sharing quiet moments in the morning. Replacing these moments with screen time reduces connection.

When rituals fade, emotional closeness fades too.

Children, work and social obligations increase digital load

Parents often use devices to manage schedules, school updates, messages and planning. Many jobs require constant email monitoring. While these uses are practical, they can gradually replace relational presence if boundaries are not in place.

The result is not intentional disconnection. It is accidental neglect.

Technology is not going away. Couples cannot eliminate phones or social media from their lives. The goal is not abstinence. The goal is awareness, balance and intention.

• • •

Setting Tech Boundaries That Protect Closeness

Healthy tech boundaries do not restrict freedom. They protect connection. Boundaries create structure so that partners can be present without distraction. They create emotional breathing room. They prevent small irritations from building into resentment.

Here are boundaries that support intimacy and reduce tension.

Choose tech free moments

Select windows during the day or week when both partners set devices aside. This might be for meals, bedtime, morning routines or certain evenings. These moments create opportunities for emotional closeness.

A simple script helps open the conversation:

I feel disconnected when we are both on our phones. Can we choose a tech free hour tonight.

This request is gentle and clear. It communicates desire for connection, not control.

Make the bedroom a connection zone

Devices in the bedroom reduce intimacy. Notifications interrupt conversations. Screens delay sleep. Social media distracts from emotional and physical closeness.

Many couples find that removing devices from the bedroom

strengthens intimacy more than any other habit. The bedroom becomes a place for rest, affection and quiet conversation.

Create a daily wind down ritual

Instead of drifting into screen time at night, create a simple ritual:

talking for a few minutes

sharing gratitude

cuddling

breathing together

listening to soft music

These habits help the nervous system settle and support connection.

Communicate openly about digital boundaries

Partners differ in their comfort with online interaction. Some feel fine when their partner chats online. Others feel insecure. What matters is discussing it openly rather than assuming.

Use questions such as:

What online behaviors feel comfortable to you.

What feels like a boundary crossing.

How can we communicate if something online creates discomfort.

These conversations prevent misunderstandings.

Turn off nonessential notifications

Notifications break presence. Many are unnecessary. Turning off nonessential alerts reduces digital noise and makes conversations more connected.

Agree on messaging habits during shared time

When couples spend time together, phone interruptions can feel disrespectful. Agree on how you will manage messages, such as:

Only answering urgent texts

Letting each other know if something important comes in

Checking phones only at agreed moments

This creates a shared digital rhythm.

Clarify expectations about social media

Partners may differ in how they use social media. They may differ in boundaries around posting, interacting with others or sharing personal details.

Talk openly about:

What feels respectful

What feels uncomfortable

What creates insecurity

What supports trust

Clarity strengthens closeness.

Protect connection at reunions

When partners come home or reconnect after time apart, a few minutes of focused presence makes a big difference. A warm greeting, a hug or a short check in creates emotional anchoring. Checking phones at this moment weakens connection.

Make reunions intentional.

Recognize when technology becomes avoidance

Sometimes people escape into digital life because they feel overwhelmed. When this happens often, the underlying issue needs attention. Talk about what is being avoided and explore how to support each other emotionally.

Avoidance is not a flaw. It is a signal.

Honor each other's requests for presence

When a partner says, I feel disconnected or I need your attention, respond with openness. These requests express vulnerability. They also reveal a desire for closeness. Dismissing them can cause deep hurt. Taking them seriously strengthens love.

How to Balance Connection with Digital Life

Total disconnection from technology is unrealistic. Phones, computers and social media are part of modern life. The goal is balance. A balanced approach integrates digital engagement with emotional presence.

Here are insights that help couples create healthy balance.

Understand your own digital habits

Before setting boundaries, reflect on your relationship with technology. Ask yourself:

Do I use my phone to avoid discomfort.

Do I check my phone out of habit rather than need.

Do I rely on social media for emotional validation.

Do I use digital noise to numb stress.

Self awareness helps you communicate more clearly.

Understand your partner's habits without judgment

Partners may cope with stress differently. One might scroll to unwind. The other might prefer silence. One might use social media socially. The other might barely use it at all.

Avoid labeling habits as good or bad. Instead, discuss how they impact connection.

Create tech agreements rather than rules

Agreements come from teamwork. Rules feel restrictive. Agreements allow negotiation and revisions. They also ensure that both partners contribute to decisions.

A script to start the conversation:

I want to protect our closeness. How can we handle messages, notifications and social media in a way that feels good for both of us.

This script keeps the conversation open and collaborative.

Use digital life to strengthen connection, not replace it

Technology can support the relationship when used intentionally. You can:

send thoughtful messages

share music or articles

send photos throughout the day

share funny or sweet videos

check in emotionally

These actions strengthen connection rather than weaken it.

Practice mindful tech use

Mindfulness means paying attention to how you feel while using technology. If you notice tension, irritation or numbness, pause. Ask yourself what you actually need. Often the need is rest, connection or calm rather than digital stimulation.

Rebuild presence through tiny rituals

Presence does not need elaborate planning. Couples can reconnect through:

eye contact

soft conversation

shared breathing

touch

quiet moments together

Technology pulls attention outward. Presence reconnects attention inward, toward the relationship.

Revisit tech agreements regularly

Life changes. Stress changes. Work demands change. Tech agreements should evolve with the couple. Revisit them every few months to see what is working and what needs adjustment.

Address deeper emotional patterns beneath tech conflict

Arguments about phones are rarely about phones. They are about:

feeling unseen

feeling second to a device

feeling insecure

feeling overwhelmed

feeling neglected

When couples address the emotional layer, tech conflict becomes easier to navigate.

Exercise: Create a Shared Tech Agreement

This exercise helps couples create boundaries that protect closeness. Complete it together.

Step 1: Share your personal experience with technology

Each partner answers:

How does technology help me.

How does it distract me.

When do I feel most disconnected because of devices.

Step 2: Identify sensitive moments

Discuss moments when tech use hurts connection, such as:

bedtime

meals

mornings

reunions

date nights

Step 3: Choose connection priorities

Identify a few moments when presence matters most.

Step 4: Choose tech free zones or times

Examples:

dining table

bedroom

first 15 minutes after reconnecting

one evening per week

Step 5: Agree on messaging boundaries

Discuss how to handle:

nonurgent messages

work communication

social media activity

Step 6: Create mutual promises

Examples:

We will check in before using phones during shared time.

We will talk openly if something online triggers insecurity.

Step 7: Write your agreement

Keep it brief, flexible and kind.

Step 8: Revisit monthly

Adjust as needed.

This agreement is not a rule book. It is a commitment to presence.

SCRIPTS FOR TECH AND PRESENCE CONVERSATIONS

Script 1: Expressing disconnection kindly

I feel disconnected when we are both on our phones. Can we choose a tech free hour tonight.

Script 2: Protecting closeness together

I want to protect our closeness. How can we handle messages, notifications and social media in a way that feels good for both of us.

Use these scripts often. They make it easier to speak up without blame.

CLOSING THOUGHTS

Technology has changed how couples relate, communicate and spend time together. It has created new opportunities for connection and new challenges for presence. Phones are not the enemy. Social media is not the enemy. The real challenge is learning how to stay emotionally connected while living in a digital environment designed to distract.

Closeness is not built from physical proximity. It is built from emotional presence. It is built from moments when partners look into each other's eyes, listen deeply, hold hands, share a story or simply exist together without distraction. When couples protect these moments, their connection becomes strong enough to handle the digital world rather than be weakened by it.

Technology will continue to evolve. Notifications will continue to pull at attention. But couples who choose presence, who create agreements, who listen to each other's needs and who protect small moments of togetherness will stay connected through every change.

Presence is love in practice. And it is possible even in a digital world.

Part 5
Staying Connected for the Long Run

Chapter 13
Creating a Shared Future

A relationship is not only built on the past you have lived or the present you are navigating. It is built on the future you imagine together. Couples who stay close for the long run share more than a home, a routine or a history. They share a direction. They share purpose. They share vision. They create a sense of us that carries them through seasons of change, stress and transition.

> The future is not a destination you reach. It is something you co create again and again. Every year, every season, every major life shift invites you to shape your partnership in new ways.

When couples talk openly about their goals, values, dreams and needs, they remain emotionally aligned. When they avoid these conversations, quiet drift begins. Drift is not dramatic. It is subtle. It comes from missed check ins, unspoken expectations, mismatched priorities and the assumption that your partner will simply know where you are headed.

Creating a shared future is not about planning everything perfectly. It is about staying close while life unfolds. It is about choosing each other again and again with intention. It is about building a partnership with room for two whole, evolving people.

This chapter explores how to create shared goals, how to balance independence with partnership and how regular check ins keep the relationship healthy. You will find a yearly relationship review template and scripts that help you speak openly about the future you want to build.

Love grows in the soil of shared vision. Let's talk about how to cultivate it.

Goals as a Couple

Every couple has goals, even if they never talk about them. Some goals are practical, like buying a home or saving money. Some are emotional, like creating a peaceful household or becoming better listeners. Some are relational, like deepening intimacy or building family traditions. Goals do not need to be grand to matter. They only need to be shared.

When couples talk about their goals, they strengthen connection in three powerful ways:

They communicate values.

They reveal inner desires.

They build teamwork.

Goals remind you that you are not just living side by side. You are building something together.

Here are the types of goals that keep relationships thriving.

Practical goals

These goals focus on the logistics of shared life.

Examples:

financial stability

career decisions

housing plans

health support

lifestyle choices

Practical goals create structure. They reduce stress because both partners understand what they are working toward.

These goals often require negotiation and compromise. One partner may want adventure while the other wants stability. One may want to invest while the other wants to enjoy life now. These differences are normal. What matters is understanding each other's emotional reasoning rather than fighting over surface preferences.

You can ask:

What is one practical goal that matters to you this year.

What makes that goal meaningful for you.

When you understand each other's reasoning, compromise becomes collaboration.

Emotional goals

Emotional goals shape the quality of the relationship itself. These are often the most important goals, yet couples rarely name them directly.

Examples:

feeling more connected

reducing conflict

improving communication

spending more time in closeness

increasing affection

supporting mental health

Emotional goals matter because relationships thrive when both partners feel emotionally nourished. If emotional goals go unmet, practical goals become harder to pursue.

You can ask:

What is one emotional shift you want for us this year.

This question opens a gentle doorway into deeper connection.

Intimacy goals

Intimacy goals include emotional closeness, physical closeness and relational depth.

Examples:

creating weekly connection rituals

improving communication during sex

increasing affection

exploring deeper intimacy

repairing past wounds

These goals help couples connect on deeper levels. Intimacy is not static. It changes with seasons, stress levels and stages of life. Naming intimacy goals keeps closeness alive.

Adventure and growth goals

These goals keep the relationship vibrant.

Examples:

travel

learning together

new hobbies

creative projects

spiritual exploration

trying new experiences

Adventure goals reinfuse the relationship with curiosity, surprise and joy. They help couples feel alive together rather than stuck in routine.

Long term goals

These include dreams about:

family

retirement

location

career direction

shared legacy

Long term goals give partners a sense of trajectory. They help couples feel like they are building a meaningful life, not just surviving day to day tasks.

Why Shared Goals Reduce Conflict

Conflict often happens when partners move in different directions without realizing it. One person pushes forward, the other pulls back, and both feel misunderstood. Shared goals reduce conflict because they create alignment.

When you know what you want as a couple, disagreements become easier to navigate. You can ask:

Does this choice support our shared direction.

Does this decision bring us closer to what we want.

Shared goals turn conflict from a power struggle into a conversation about alignment.

Goals are not rigid rules. They are guiding stars. They keep you pointed in the same direction, even when life gets hectic.

Balancing Independence and Partnership

A healthy long term relationship requires both togetherness and individuality. Too much merging can smother growth. Too much independence can create distance. The balance shifts through life. What matters is awareness and communication.

Here are the key principles of balancing independence and partnership.

Strong relationships include two whole people

Partnership is not about becoming the same person or doing everything together. It is about supporting each other's individuality while building a shared life. When both partners stay connected to their own hobbies, passions, friendships and personal goals, the relationship remains vibrant.

Healthy independence strengthens the relationship because each partner continues to grow.

Independence is not emotional distance

Some people confuse independence with withdrawal. Independence is pursuing personal growth while staying emotionally available. Withdrawal is pulling away to avoid connection.

Healthy independence says:

I love exploring my interests and I bring my energy back to us.

Unhealthy withdrawal says:

I avoid connection because it feels overwhelming or uncomfortable.

The difference is presence.

Partnership is not control

Some partners feel anxious when the other pursues independent activities. They worry that distance means disinterest. They fear losing closeness. These fears are important to acknowledge. But partnership cannot thrive if independence is restricted.

The goal is not to prevent independence. The goal is to support independence while maintaining emotional closeness through communication.

You can ask:

How can we stay connected even while doing our own things.

This question prevents independence from becoming distance.

Balance requires rhythm

Relationships go through cycles. Sometimes the couple needs more togetherness. Sometimes individuals need more personal space. Balance comes from checking in regularly rather than assuming needs will stay constant.

A simple question helps:

Where are you emotionally right now. Do you need closeness or space.

Answering this openly builds trust.

Shared life choices require mutual respect

When making major decisions such as moving, career changes or financial planning, both partners must consider each other's needs and values. Independence in goals is healthy, but major life decisions must be made with partnership in mind.

Balance means honoring your partner's dreams while also honoring your own.

Celebrate each other's growth

When your partner grows individually, the relationship grows. Supporting each other's projects, learning, passions and self development strengthens the bond. It creates pride, admiration and emotional closeness.

You can say:

What support do you need from me in this season of life.

This shows respect for your partner's journey.

Regular Check Ins That Keep the Relationship Healthy

Relationships weaken when partners stop checking in. People assume everything is fine because there are no big conflicts. But emotional distance does not appear suddenly. It appears quietly through lack of communication, unmet needs and missed opportunities for closeness.

Regular check ins prevent drift. They create a rhythm of awareness and honesty. They strengthen emotional safety.

Here are the types of check ins that help couples stay connected.

Weekly check ins

A weekly check in is short and simple. It keeps partners aligned emotionally.

You can ask:

What felt good between us this week.

What felt challenging.

What can we do next week to feel more connected.

These conversations reduce resentment and build teamwork.

Monthly check ins

Monthly check ins explore deeper patterns. They help partners reflect on:

stress

intimacy

presence

communication

support

goals

You can ask:

What have you been needing more of from me.

What have you appreciated lately.

Monthly check ins nourish emotional intimacy.

Seasonal check ins

Every season brings different energy, stress and needs. A seasonal check in helps couples evaluate how life circumstances are affecting the relationship.

Questions might include:

What has been shifting for you lately.

Is there something you want to focus on this season.

What would make life feel smoother for us right now.

Seasonal conversations create flexibility and understanding.

Yearly relationship reviews

A yearly review helps partners reflect on the entire relationship landscape.

You review your growth, your challenges, your goals and your direction. This ritual strengthens long term vision and connection.

A yearly review is like giving your relationship a tune up. It prevents small cracks from becoming larger ruptures.

The template appears later in this chapter.

Real time emotional check ins

Not all check ins need structure. Some are spontaneous and simple. They happen during daily life.

Examples:

You seem quiet. Are you okay.

I miss you today. Can we connect for a moment.

How are you feeling about us this week.

Spontaneous check ins keep the relationship warm and responsive.

Why Check Ins Strengthen Long Term Love

Check ins support:

emotional clarity

prevention of resentment

deepening communication

faster repair after misunderstandings

alignment of goals

mutual appreciation

growth and learning

Couples who check in regularly stay close even through stress or life transitions. They understand each other better and adapt more easily to change.

Check ins send a powerful message:

Our relationship matters.

Your feelings matter.

I want to understand you.

That message alone keeps love alive.

Exercise: Yearly Relationship Review Template

Use this exercise once a year. Choose a quiet day or evening. Bring warmth, curiosity and honesty. This is not an evaluation. It is a moment of shared reflection.

Part 1: Looking back

1 What were our highlights as a couple this year.

2 What challenges did we face and how did we handle them.

3 What did we learn about each other.

4 What did we learn about ourselves.

5 What are we proud of in our relationship.

Part 2: Emotional connection

1 When did we feel most connected.

2 When did we feel disconnected.

3 What helped us reconnect.

4 What emotional habits strengthened us.

5 What emotional habits created tension.

Part 3: Intimacy and closeness

1 What felt nourishing in our intimacy.

2 What felt difficult or avoided.

3 What do we want to explore next year.

Part 4: Practical life

1 What worked well in our routines, tasks and responsibilities.

2 What needs adjustment.

3 What financial or practical goals matter to us this year.

Part 5: Individual growth

1 What personal goals did each of us pursue.

2 How can we support each other's growth next year.

3 What support do you need from me in this season of life.

Part 6: Dreams and future goals

1 What is something we can build together this year.

2 What experiences do we want to create.

3 What long term goals feel important right now.

Part 7: Closing the review

Each partner shares:

One appreciation from the past year.

One hope for the coming year.

One promise for how they want to show up.

End with closeness, gratitude or affection.

This template strengthens long term connection and creates a shared direction that feels supportive for both partners.

SCRIPTS FOR FUTURE FOCUSED CONVERSATIONS

Script 1: Exploring shared goals

What is something we can build together this year.

Script 2: Supporting each other's journey

What support do you need from me in this season of life.

These scripts help partners move gently into deeper conversations about direction, purpose and emotional needs.

Staying connected for the long run is not about never arguing or never changing. It is about returning to each other with intention. It is about choosing curiosity over assumption, communication over silence and teamwork over isolation. Each year brings new challenges and new opportunities. Couples who thrive are not the ones with perfect compatibility. They are the ones who talk about their needs, share their dreams and adjust their path together.

A relationship is a living system. It grows through attention. It strengthens through shared purpose. It deepens through honest reflection. You and your partner are not just partners in the present. You are partners in the future you are building. That future does not arrive fully formed. It is shaped one conversation, one decision and one check in at a time.

When you create a shared vision, you create a shared home in time. A home made of hope, intention and love.

Chapter 14
When You Need Outside Help

Relationships are living systems. They grow, shift, stretch and sometimes struggle. Even the healthiest couples face seasons when communication becomes tangled, when emotions run high, when old patterns return or when life changes faster than the relationship can adapt. These moments are not signs of failure. They are signs that the relationship is asking for support.

Every couple reaches a point where the tools they have feel too small for the problem they are facing. This is normal. Humans are complex.

Love is complex.

Communication patterns are shaped by decades of learning. It is natural that some challenges require guidance, structure or an outside perspective.

Seeking help is not a sign that the relationship is broken. It is a sign that the relationship matters enough to protect.

Couples who seek support early tend to grow stronger and more connected than couples who wait until resentment or disconnection becomes deeply entrenched.

This chapter explores when couples should consider therapy, coaching or mediation, how to bring up the topic without shaming and how outside help can strengthen teamwork and growth. The goal is not to convince every couple to seek support. The goal is to normalize it. To remove shame. To help couples recognize that asking for help is a wise, loving and proactive choice.

Outside support is not the last resort. It is a doorway to deeper understanding,stronger communication and renewed closeness.

When a Couple Should Consider Therapy, Coaching or Mediation

Not every relationship challenge requires professional help, but many benefit greatly from it. Outside support can provide structure, clarity and emotional safety that is difficult to access during conflict.

Here are common signs that outside support would be helpful.

You have the same argument repeatedly

If you find yourselves looping through the same fight with slightly different details, it usually means the real issue is deeper than the topic on the surface. A professional can help uncover the emotional roots and teach new ways to communicate.

Small disagreements escalate quickly

Frequent escalation is a sign that your nervous systems are getting overwhelmed. A therapist or coach can help you learn calming strategies, communication tools and conflict patterns that reduce intensity.

You avoid certain topics out of fear or exhaustion

When topics like sex, money or family cause anxiety or shutdown, outside help provides a safe space to explore these conversations with guidance.

One or both partners feel lonely inside the relationship

Loneliness within a relationship often indicates emotional disconnection. Support can help rebuild intimacy, understanding and closeness.

Trust has been shaken and repair feels too hard to do alone

After secrecy, betrayal or emotional rupture, partners may feel unsure how to rebuild trust. A skilled professional can guide honest conversations and create structure for healing.

. . .

One partner feels unheard or overwhelmed

If one partner carries emotional labor or feels misunderstood, outside help can rebalance communication and support fairness.

You feel stuck and cannot find forward movement

Feeling stuck does not mean the relationship is failing. It means you are at a growth edge. Guidance provides momentum and clarity.

Individual stress is affecting the relationship

Mental health struggles, grief, burnout, work stress or major transitions can all strain connection. Support helps couples navigate the emotional load together rather than separately.

You want to grow, strengthen or improve the relationship even if nothing is wrong

Some couples use therapy or coaching proactively. They want more closeness, better communication or a shared vision. Support helps them deepen the relationship they already enjoy.

You love each other but do not know how to communicate well

This is extremely common. Love is not enough to guarantee strong communication. Skills, awareness and structure matter.

Outside help gives couples the tools they were never taught.

How to Approach the Topic Without Shaming

Bringing up therapy or coaching can feel awkward or frightening. Some people fear it sounds like criticism. They worry their partner will feel blamed or judged. But when approached gently, the topic can be an invitation, not an accusation.

Here are ways to introduce the idea with warmth and care.

Speak from love, not frustration

Begin with appreciation or reassurance. Let your partner know the relationship matters.

A soft script is:

I love us and I want extra support so we can grow through this.

This frames the conversation around growth rather than failure.

Focus on teamwork, not blame

Make it clear that you are suggesting support for both of you, not pointing to your partner as the problem.

Examples:

I think we could benefit from learning some new tools together.

I want us to feel even more connected and supported.

This removes defensiveness.

Emphasize curiosity instead of crisis

You can say:

I want to explore this to understand each other better.

I think guidance could help us grow in ways we cannot do alone.

Curiosity feels safe. Crisis feels scary.

Share your personal feelings, not accusations

You can express your emotional state without blaming.

Examples:

I sometimes feel stuck, and I want help navigating this with you.

I want to understand myself and our patterns better.

Personal language reduces tension.

Invite, do not pressure

Make it a gentle invitation.

Can we try a few sessions together and see how it feels.

This way, your partner feels free to say yes without feeling forced.

Address fears with compassion

Some people hesitate because they fear being exposed, judged or blamed. Validate these feelings.

Examples:

I know it can feel vulnerable to ask for help.

I know this might feel uncomfortable at first.

Validation shows you understand the emotional stakes.

Choose timing carefully

Do not bring up therapy during an argument or emotional storm. Choose a calm moment when both partners can listen openly.

Acknowledge that seeking help is normal

Normalize the process.

Lots of strong couples seek support. It does not mean anything is wrong with us. It means we want to strengthen what we have.

Normalizing reduces shame.

What Therapy, Coaching or Mediation Provides

Professional support offers several things that are difficult to access when you are stuck inside the relationship patterns.

Structure

A therapist or coach guides conversations so they do not escalate or spiral. This structure helps each partner feel heard and understood. It also helps couples stay focused on the emotional root rather than getting lost in surface details.

Emotional safety

Professionals create a calm and contained space where both partners can express feelings without interruption or judgment. This safety helps couples say things they have avoided saying.

A neutral perspective

When you are inside the relationship, it can be difficult to see your patterns clearly. An outside observer identifies patterns you may not have noticed and helps you shift them.

New communication tools

Many couples simply were never taught how to communicate well. Professionals teach skills for listening, expressing needs, de escalation, conflict repair and intimacy.

These skills last a lifetime.

Support for rebuilding trust

Guided conversations help couples understand what caused trust rupture and how to rebuild it step by step with clarity, honesty and consistency.

Insight into emotional triggers and patterns

Therapy helps partners understand their emotional histories, attachment patterns, defenses and coping mechanisms. This awareness transforms communication.

Hope and direction

Outside support gives couples a roadmap. It turns confusion into clarity and overwhelm into manageable steps.

. . .

Encouraging Growth as a Team

Seeking outside help is not about fixing one person. It is about strengthening the couple as a team. Growth happens when both partners feel supported and motivated.

Here are ways to encourage growth together.

Create shared goals for the support process

Examples:

communicate more calmly

rebuild trust

create more intimacy

reduce conflict

understand each other better

develop emotional tools

Having shared goals increases motivation and reduces fear.

Celebrate small growth moments

Not every breakthrough will be dramatic. Sometimes growth looks like:

talking more calmly

pausing before reacting

listening with more presence

repairing more quickly

expressing needs clearly

Celebrate these moments. They show progress.

Stay compassionate with yourselves

Growth is uncomfortable. It reveals raw places, old wounds and emotional patterns. Compassion softens defensiveness. It also helps couples stay patient with the process.

Use what you learn outside of sessions

Practice the tools in daily life. Review insights together. Try new communication habits. Let the support experience enrich your relationship, not stay isolated in a weekly session.

Stay flexible as new layers emerge

Sometimes therapy reveals unexpected emotions or patterns. Approach these with openness.

You can say:

We are learning a lot, and I want to stay with you through this.

Flexibility allows deeper transformation.

Recognize that vulnerability creates closeness

Sharing fears, mistakes, longings and needs builds intimacy. The healing process itself becomes a bonding experience.

Commit to the long view

Growing together takes time. Support is not a quick fix. But each step builds a more resilient, connected and emotionally literate relationship.

Exercise: Self Assessment Checklist

Do We Need Professional Support?**

Use this checklist honestly and gently. Check any statements that feel true.

Communication patterns

We argue about the same things repeatedly.

We struggle to stay calm during difficult conversations.

We avoid certain topics because they feel too stressful.

We talk but do not feel understood.

One of us shuts down or withdraws during conflict.

We have trouble listening without interrupting.

Emotional connection

We feel more like roommates than partners.

One or both of us feel lonely in the relationship.

We struggle to reconnect after tension.

We carry resentment that has not been fully discussed.

Trust and safety

Past hurts still affect us.

There is secrecy we have not resolved.

There has been a betrayal that still feels unresolved.

Intimacy

Our physical or emotional intimacy feels distant or stuck.

We avoid talking about intimacy because it feels confusing or painful.

Stress

External stress is affecting the relationship.

One or both of us feel overwhelmed and unsupported.

Growth

We want better communication skills.

We want support in creating a shared future.

We want help understanding each other more deeply.

If you checked several boxes, outside help could be a meaningful step.

This is not a sign of failure. It is a sign that you care about the relationship enough to strengthen it.

SCRIPTS FOR BEGINNING THE CONVERSATION

Script 1: Loving invitation

I love us and I want extra support so we can grow through this.

Script 2: Gentle suggestion

Can we try a few sessions together and see how it feels.

These scripts invite openness rather than defensiveness.

Every relationship faces moments of confusion, tension or emotional overwhelm. These moments do not mean the relationship is broken. They mean the relationship is alive. Growth is not a straight line. Sometimes couples need a guide, a witness, a teacher or a facilitator to help them move forward.

Seeking help is not about weakness. It is about strength. It is about choosing the relationship with maturity, humility and love. It is about saying, Our connection matters enough to invest in. It is about acknowledging that two loving people still have blind spots and still need support.

Outside help gives couples tools they can use for the rest of their lives. It increases emotional intelligence, deepens intimacy and strengthens trust. It creates a shared language for communication. It transforms confusion into clarity and distance into closeness.

If your relationship needs support, consider reaching for it now. You deserve tools that help you love more deeply, communicate more clearly and grow more fully. Your partnership deserves a future shaped with intention, not fear.

Asking for help is an act of love. It is one of the strongest choices a couple can make.

Part 6
Workbook Appendix

Practical Tools for Daily Connection

This appendix gathers the core exercises from the book into a simple, easy to use workbook format. Couples can use these pages weekly, seasonally or whenever they want to reconnect. Each exercise is laid out with clear prompts and generous space for reflection.

These pages turn insight into action and conversation into connection.

Emotional Safety and Communication Foundations

Exercise 1: Your Personal Triggers and Calming Plan

Step 1: Identify your three most common triggers

1.

2.

3.

Step 2: What do these triggers remind you of or touch inside you

1.

2.

3.

Step 3: Calming strategies that help you stay present

deep breathing

short pause

kind self talk

grounding touch

movement or stretching

quiet space

Write the ones that work best for you:

My calming plan:

1.

2.

3.

Step 4: Words you can use when feeling overwhelmed

I need a moment to breathe so I can come back and listen better.

I feel myself getting activated. Can we pause for a minute.

Write a phrase that feels natural for you:

Exercise 2: Five Minute Mirror and Repeat Practice

Use this to improve listening.

Speaker:

Talk for two minutes about something on your mind.

Listener:

Reflect back:

What I hear you saying is... Did I get that right.

Switch roles.

Notes about what felt helpful:

Notes about what felt difficult:

Exercise 3: Turning a Complaint into a Need Statement

Choose a recent frustration and rewrite it.

Complaint:

Underlying feeling:

Underlying need:

Need statement:

When X happened, I felt Y, and what I need is Z.

Write yours here:

Understanding Patterns and Triggers

Exercise 4: Identify Your Three Flash Points

Flash point 1:

What happened externally:

What it brought up internally:

Flash point 2:

External:

Internal:

Flash point 3:

External:

Internal:

Exercise 5: Connection Style Quiz (Short Version)

Mark the statements that feel most true.

Reassurance seeking style:

I worry about losing closeness.

I want more communication than my partner offers.

Disconnect feels very painful for me.

Space seeking style:

I feel overwhelmed when emotions run high.

I need time alone to process.

I pull back when I am unsure what I feel.

Steady style:

I feel generally secure.

I can balance closeness and space.

I try to stay calm even during difficulty.

Reflection:

My primary pattern seems to be:

What this pattern looks like under stress:

What I want my partner to understand about it:

Conflict and Repair Skills

Exercise 6: Conflict De Escalation Map

Step 1: Notice early signs of escalation

racing thoughts

tight chest

anger rising

shutting down

Write yours:

Step 2: Choose a pause strategy

short timeout

slowing your voice

naming the feeling

Write your pause plan:

Step 3: Join the team again

Use a phrase such as:

I want us to pause. I am on your side.

Write a phrase that feels natural for you:

Step 4: Identify shared goals

What part of this do we both care about.

Daily and Deep Connection Practices

Exercise 7: Weekly Ritual of Connection

Plan one ritual you will practice together.

What day and time will it happen:

What you will do:

talking

walking

cuddling

weekly review

date night

coffee ritual

How long it will last:

What both partners hope to gain from it:

Exercise 8: Twenty Questions for Deeper Bonding

Pick three questions per week or use all twenty during a retreat.

1 What is one hope you have for the coming year.

2 What helps you feel most supported by me.

3 What scares you about the future.

4 What excites you about the future.

5 What is something you wish I understood more deeply.

6 What dreams have you put aside that you want to revisit.

7 How has love changed you.

8 What are you learning about yourself lately.

9 What do you find beautiful about our relationship.

10 When do you feel closest to me.

11 What kind of intimacy nourishes you most.

12 What part of our relationship feels strongest right now.

13 What part feels tender or uncertain.

14 What support do you want in this season of life.

15 What helps you feel emotionally safe.

16 How can we repair more gently after conflict.

17 What is a dream we have not talked about yet.

18 What do you appreciate about me that you rarely say out loud.

19 What memories do you cherish most from our time together.

20 What vision do you have for our relationship five years from now.

Space for notes:

Intimacy and Trust Healing Tools

Exercise 7: Weekly Ritual of Connection

Plan one ritual you will practice together.

What day and time will it happen:

What you will do:

talking

walking

cuddling

weekly review

date night

coffee ritual

How long it will last:

What both partners hope to gain from it:

Exercise 8: Twenty Questions for Deeper Bonding

Pick three questions per week or use all twenty during a retreat.

1 What is one hope you have for the coming year.

2 What helps you feel most supported by me.

3 What scares you about the future.

4 What excites you about the future.

5 What is something you wish I understood more deeply.

6 What dreams have you put aside that you want to revisit.

7 How has love changed you.

8 What are you learning about yourself lately.

9 What do you find beautiful about our relationship.

10 When do you feel closest to me.

11 What kind of intimacy nourishes you most.

12 What part of our relationship feels strongest right now.

13 What part feels tender or uncertain.

14 What support do you want in this season of life.

15 What helps you feel emotionally safe.

16 How can we repair more gently after conflict.

17 What is a dream we have not talked about yet.

18 What do you appreciate about me that you rarely say out loud.

19 What memories do you cherish most from our time together.

20 What vision do you have for our relationship five years from now.

Space for notes:

Technology, Presence and Balance

Exercise 11: Shared Tech Agreement

Part 1: What helps me feel connected

Part 2: What disconnects me

Part 3: Sensitive moments where tech gets in the way

Part 4: Our tech free zones or times

Part 5: How we handle messages and notifications

Part 6: Agreements that support closeness

Future Planning and Long Term Connection

Exercise 12: Yearly Relationship Review

Looking back

Highlights:

Challenges:

Lessons:

Emotional connection

Moments of closeness:

Moments of distance:

Intimacy

What felt nourishing:

What felt difficult:

Practical life

What worked well:

What needs adjusting:

Looking forward

What is something we want to build together this year:

What support do we need from each other:

Seven Day Connection Reset Worksheets

Every relationship benefits from small moments of intention. We often assume closeness grows naturally, but closeness grows because partners choose to nurture it. This book has given you tools to communicate clearly, listen deeply, understand patterns, repair conflict, talk about difficult topics and create a shared future. Now it is time to give your relationship something simple and immediately usable. A structure you can start today. A short reset that brings you closer without overwhelm.

The Seven Day Connection Reset is designed to help couples reconnect gently and steadily. It is not a complicated program. It does not require hours of work. Each day focuses on one element of healthy communication and intimacy. The practice takes about ten to twenty minutes. Some couples use it as a starting point, others revisit it at every anniversary, season change or moment of drift. It is meant to be a gift to your relationship, one that is easy to begin and meaningful to complete.

This weeklong reset helps couples shift from habit to intention, from autopilot to presence, from disconnection to closeness. You will be guided through daily themes that reflect the core teachings of this book: appreciation, listening, expressing needs, repair, intimacy, planning and vision.

Consider this chapter the bridge between learning and living. A reset that invites you to step back into connection with clarity, kindness and hope.

Let us begin.

How to Use This Seven Day Reset

You and your partner can complete each day at the same time or whenever it works. You may want to choose a quiet moment in the evening or a calm moment in the morning. Turn off notifications. Sit close. Bring curiosity. Bring warmth. Bring willingness.

There is no grading here. There is no right or wrong. If a day feels emotional, go slowly. If you miss a day, simply continue the next. What matters is not perfection. What matters is presence.

Each day includes:

a simple practice

a short conversation prompt

a moment of connection

These practices help you reconnect without pressure.

Day 1: Appreciation

Appreciation is one of the most powerful habits in a relationship. It softens tension, builds warmth and reminds partners why they chose each other. Appreciation is the antidote to negativity. When you name what you value, you strengthen the emotional foundation of your relationship.

Many couples stop expressing appreciation because they assume it is obvious. Yet no one is ever harmed by hearing they are valued. Appreciation restores emotional safety and opens hearts for the week ahead.

Practice

Sit together and share three things you appreciated about each other in the past few days. Be specific and sincere.

Examples:

I appreciated how patient you were when I felt overwhelmed.

I appreciated your humor this morning. It lifted my mood.

I appreciated how you handled things at home while I was busy.

Avoid mixing appreciation with suggestions. Keep it pure.

Discussion Prompt

Ask each other:

What kind of appreciation helps you feel most loved.

Connection Moment

Hold hands. Take a slow breath together. Let the warmth settle.

Appreciation begins the reset by creating emotional safety.

Day 2: Listening

Listening is the foundation of understanding. Most people listen to respond rather than to understand. Today is about slowing down, offering full attention and reflecting back what your partner shares.

Listening says, I choose to know you. It strengthens closeness immediately.

Practice

Choose one partner to speak for two or three minutes about something on their mind. It does not need to be deep or dramatic. It could be a stressor, a thought, a memory or anything they want to share. The listener practices presence. No fixing. No debating. Just listening.

Then the listener reflects:

What I hear you saying is… Did I get that right.

Then switch roles.

Discussion Prompt

Ask each other:

When do you feel most heard by me.

Connection Moment

Look at your partner for a moment without words. Presence is the gift today.

Listening softens defenses and rebuilds emotional closeness.

Day 3: Needs

Closeness depends on the ability to express needs clearly and kindly. Many conflicts grow from unspoken needs that turn into frustration. Today focuses on speaking honestly without blame.

Needs are not demands. They are invitations for understanding.

Practice

Each partner shares one need using this structure:

When X happened, I felt Y, and what I need is Z.

Examples:

When the week gets busy, I feel overwhelmed, and what I need is more shared planning.

When we are quiet for long periods, I feel distant, and what I need is a few minutes of connection.

The listener responds with curiosity, not defensiveness.

Discussion Prompt

Ask each other:

What is one emotional need you want me to understand more clearly.

Connection Moment

Place a hand on each other's chest or back. Breathe slowly. Needs are about connection, not pressure.

Honest needs strengthen trust and reduce resentment.

Day 4: Repair

Every couple experiences tension. What matters most is how quickly and kindly they return to each other after conflict. Repair is not about blame. It is about understanding and reconnection.

Today is a gentle moment to practice repair even if nothing is wrong. By practicing during calm times, you build the skill for harder moments.

Practice

Each partner shares something small that felt off, tense or confusing recently, using warm language.

Examples:

I felt sad when we were disconnected the other night.

I felt tense when we rushed through that conversation.

The other partner responds with empathy:

I see how that affected you. Thank you for telling me.

Then each partner completes one small repair:

I am sorry for my part in that.

Here is what I will try next time.

Discussion Prompt

Ask each other:

What helps you feel safe during repair.

Connection Moment

Offer a gentle touch, a hug or a quiet moment together. Repair brings hearts close again.

Repair is a skill. Practicing it strengthens resilience.

Day 5: Intimacy

Intimacy includes emotional closeness, physical closeness and the feeling of being seen. Today is not necessarily about sexual intimacy, although it may lead to that if both partners feel comfortable. It is about opening the heart.

Intimacy grows when partners feel safe, curious and willing to share.

Practice

Each partner shares:

Here is what helps me feel emotionally close to you.

Here is what helps me feel physically close to you.

Be gentle, personal and honest. Speak without pressure.

Examples:

I feel close when we have slow conversations without distraction.

I feel close when you touch my back or hold my hand.

Discussion Prompt

Ask each other:

What is one small thing we could do more often to increase intimacy.

Connection Moment

Sit close. Place a hand on each other's thigh, arm or shoulder. Hold the moment without rushing.

Intimacy deepens when partners choose to be present and vulnerable.

Day 6: Planning

A relationship grows stronger when partners look ahead together. Planning does not need to be intense. It simply means choosing a shared direction.

Today is about dreaming, organizing and aligning, even in small ways. When couples plan together, they feel like a team.

Practice

Discuss one short term goal for the next month and one long term goal for the next year.

Ask each other:

What is something we can build together this year.

This might include:

a communication habit

a financial goal

a creative project

a health habit

a family plan

a personal growth goal

The key is collaboration.

Discussion Prompt

Ask:

How can we support each other's goals individually and as a couple.

Connection Moment

Picture something you want to build together. Share a smile or a hopeful thought.

Planning builds direction and strengthens partnership.

Day 7: Celebration and Future Vision

Celebration strengthens connection by recognizing progress. Vision strengthens connection by giving the relationship a future. Today is about naming what you love, honoring your growth and imagining what you want next.

This final day is both reflective and forward looking.

Practice

Share three things you appreciated about this seven day reset.

Examples:

I loved our slow conversations.

I felt closer when we practiced listening.

I appreciated how honest you were about your needs.

Then share one vision for the future:

Something you hope to experience

Something you want to build

Something you want to nurture

Discussion Prompt

Ask each other:

What do you want our relationship to feel like this coming year.

Connection Moment

Hold each other. Breathe together. End the week with shared presence.

This final day seals the reset with gratitude and hope.

Why This Seven Day Reset Works

This reset works because it highlights the emotional building blocks of closeness.

Day 1 warms the connection through appreciation.

Day 2 strengthens understanding through listening.

Day 3 builds honesty and clarity through needs.

Day 4 deepens resilience through repair.

Day 5 expands closeness through intimacy.

Day 6 aligns goals through planning.

Day 7 celebrates growth through vision.

Each day activates one essential skill of healthy partnership. Together, they form a loop of connection that couples can return to any time they feel distant or overwhelmed.

Connection is not mysterious. It is built through intention. When couples spend even a few minutes each day nurturing their bond, everything becomes easier. Communication softens. Tension becomes manageable. Intimacy deepens. Appreciation grows. Hope returns.

This reset is a gentle invitation to begin again, no matter how long you have been together or what you have faced. Love grows through practice. Your relationship deserves that practice.

Closing Words

Thank you for completing this journey. This book has offered tools for listening, speaking, repairing, planning and staying close through every season of life. The Seven Day Connection Reset brings these tools into action. It is a reminder that love is not something we simply feel. It is something we practice every day.

Whether you are starting fresh, rebuilding after difficulty or strengthening an already beautiful bond, the skills you have learned here can guide you for years to come. Use them gently. Use them consistently. Return to them often.

Love remains steady when partners choose connection again and again. Let this reset be your invitation to continue choosing each other, with clarity, presence and kindness.

You are building something meaningful. Keep going.

Seven Day Connection Reset Worksheets

Seven Day Connection Reset Worksheets**

Use these after completing the final chapter.

Day 1: Appreciation

Three things I appreciated about you:

1.

2.

3.

How it felt to share this:

Day 2: Listening

What I heard from you today:

What felt healing about being heard:

Day 3: Needs

My need statement for today:

Your response that helped me feel understood:

Day 4: Repair

What felt tender or unresolved:

What I learned from hearing your experience:

What we each commit to:

Day 5: Intimacy

What helps me feel emotionally close:

What helps me feel physically close:

One small intimacy habit we want to add:

Day 6: Planning

Short term goal:

Long term goal:

How we will support each other:

Day 7: Celebration and Future Vision

Three things I loved about this reset:

1.

2.

3.

My vision for us:

The 30 Day Connection Journey

A deep and lasting relationship is not built in a single conversation or during a single week of effort. It grows through small, intentional practices repeated over time. Many couples want to strengthen their bond but feel unsure where to begin. They want more affection, more communication, more intimacy and more teamwork, yet daily life makes these intentions difficult to sustain.

The 30 Day Connection Journey offers a gentle, structured path that helps couples grow closer one day at a time. Each day includes one small action or short conversation that takes only a few minutes but builds emotional intimacy in powerful ways. This journey is not about perfection or pressure. It is about presence. It is about choosing each other again and again.

This chapter expands the core ideas of the book and turns them into daily habits. Completing the journey will help you and your partner strengthen attachment, deepen understanding, increase emotional safety and renew closeness. Many couples use this journey at the start of a new year, after a challenging season, before a big life transition or simply because they want to feel more connected.

Take this journey slowly. Be gentle with yourself and with each other. Bring curiosity, warmth and kindness. What matters most is not getting every day perfect. What matters is showing up.

How to Use the 30 Day Journey

Each day has:

a theme

a short practice

a prompt to explore

a moment of shared presence

You can do each task in ten to twenty minutes. Some days may inspire longer conversations, but there is no obligation to make them long. Let the process feel natural and inviting.

Choose a time of day when you are both relaxed. Evening often works well. Turn off notifications. Sit close. Let this be a ritual.

At the end of 30 days you will have woven dozens of micro moments of connection into your relationship. These moments build warmth, trust and closeness that remain long after the journey ends.

Day 1-30

Week One: Rebuilding the Emotional Foundation

The first week focuses on emotional safety, warmth and understanding. These practices prepare the relationship for deeper work in the following weeks.

Day 1: A Soft Start

Begin gently.

Practice:

Share one thing you appreciated today. Keep it small and pure.

Prompt:

What do you need tonight to feel relaxed and connected.

Presence Moment:

Hold hands or place a hand on each other's arm for one slow breath.

Day 2: Curiosity Without Fixing

Curiosity creates connection. Fixing creates distance. Today you practice listening with pure interest.

Practice:

Ask your partner one simple question:

What was something that made your day easier or harder today.

Listen without offering solutions.

Prompt:

When do you feel most understood by me.

Presence Moment:

Make three seconds of eye contact before ending the conversation.

Day 3: Naming Feelings Kindly

Today you name emotions without shame or judgment.

Practice:

Each partner shares one feeling from the past week and why it mattered.

Prompt:

What helps you feel safe sharing your emotions with me.

Presence Moment:

Offer a warm touch, even light contact on the shoulder.

Day 4: Sharing a Personal Story

Understanding grows when partners learn each other's histories.

Practice:

Share a brief story from your childhood that shaped who you are.

Prompt:

How does that story still affect your reactions or needs today.

Presence Moment:

Thank each other for trusting the space.

Day 5: The Appreciation Stretch

Today you stretch beyond basic appreciation.

Practice:

Share one appreciation about something your partner does and one about who they are.

Prompt:

What do you wish I appreciated more often.

Presence Moment:

Smile at each other. A real, slow smile.

Day 6: Speaking a Gentle Need

Needs are invitations for closeness.

Practice:

Each partner uses the simple structure:

Something that would help me feel close this week is…

Prompt:

What makes it hard for you to share needs sometimes.

Presence Moment:

A slow exhale together.

Day 7: The Emotional Temperature Check

Think of today as a small relationship tune up.

Practice:

Rate how connected you have felt this week from one to ten. Share why.

Prompt:

What would help raise that number by just one point.

Presence Moment:

Thank your partner for sharing honestly.

Week Two: Deepening Understanding

This week builds emotional intimacy, empathy and clear communication.

Day 8: The Listening Switch

Today you practice switching roles smoothly.

Practice:

One partner speaks for two minutes. The other reflects. Switch.

Prompt:

What made listening easy or hard today.

Presence Moment:

Share one gentle affirmation.

Day 9: Exploring Emotional Triggers

Understanding triggers increases compassion.

Practice:

Each partner names one small trigger from the week and the memory or feeling beneath it.

Prompt:

How can I support you when that trigger appears.

Presence Moment:

Place a hand on your partner's back or shoulder for reassurance.

Day 10: A Fear and a Hope

Sharing both vulnerability and optimism strengthens connection.

Practice:

Share one fear about the future and one hope.

Prompt:

What helps you feel secure in uncertainty.

Presence Moment:

Hold both hands for one slow breath.

Day 11: What Closeness Means to You

Today you define intimacy in your own words.

Practice:

Each partner completes:

I feel close to you when...

Prompt:

What small habit helps you feel seen.

Presence Moment:

Lean your shoulders together.

Day 12: The Compassion Script

Compassion softens defenses.

Practice:

Say to your partner:

I see how that would feel difficult.

or

Your feelings make sense to me.

Prompt:

What kind of compassion feels most comforting.

Presence Moment:

Exchange a warm look before ending the conversation.

Day 13: The Unspoken Thought

We often carry thoughts we never share.

Practice:

Share one thought you had this week that you did not say out loud.

Prompt:

What stops you from saying those things in the moment.

Presence Moment:

A gentle touch on the forearm or hand.

Day 14: A Moment You Felt Loved

Love is felt in small ways.

Practice:

Describe one moment this week when you felt loved or supported.

Prompt:

How can I offer more of that.

Presence Moment:

Thank your partner for the way they show love.

Week Three: Intimacy, Repair and Trust

This week nurtures the deeper layers of partnership.

Day 15: Your Intimacy Map

Intimacy begins with understanding.

Practice:

Share three things that help you feel emotionally close and three that help physical closeness feel safe.

Prompt:

What helps you relax into intimacy.

Presence Moment:

Sit close and breathe deeply.

Day 16: Honest Apologies

Even small moments of tension deserve gentle repair.

Practice:

Each partner identifies something small from the past week and offers a sincere apology.

Prompt:

What makes an apology feel real to you.

Presence Moment:

A soft hug or forehead touch.

Day 17: Listening to Hurt Without Defensiveness

Being heard without interruption heals wounds.

Practice:

Each partner shares one small hurt while the other listens.

Use:

I can see that this affected you.

Prompt:

What helps you feel safe sharing hurt.

Presence Moment:

Hold hands quietly.

Day 18: Rebuilding Trust in Small Steps

Trust grows through consistency.

Practice:

Share one action that would help you feel more secure.

Prompt:

What does reliability look like for you in daily life.

Presence Moment:

A reassuring touch or warm smile.

Day 19: Removing One Small Barrier to Intimacy

Every relationship has small blocks.

Practice:

Name a small habit that creates distance. Choose one to soften this week.

Prompt:

How can we support each other in this change.

Presence Moment:

A slow breath together.

Day 20: A Shared Memory Review

Remembering good times strengthens connection.

Practice:

Each partner describes one favorite memory with the other.

Prompt:

What did that moment teach you about our relationship.

Presence Moment:

Look at each other and savor the memory.

Day 21: The Trust Reassurance Ritual

Trust needs nourishment.

Practice:

Speak a reassurance statement such as:

I am here with you.

or

I want to keep growing with you.

Prompt:

What reassurance helps you feel anchored.

Presence Moment:

Lean close, letting the reassurance settle.

Week Four: Planning, Alignment and Future Vision

This final week strengthens partnership for the long run.

Day 22: The Life Logistics Check In

Practical clarity reduces stress.

Practice:

Discuss schedules, responsibilities and upcoming stress points calmly.

Prompt:

Is there a way we can make next week smoother for each other.

Presence Moment:

A shared nod or gentle smile.

Day 23: Supporting Each Other's Personal Growth

Strong couples celebrate individuality.

Practice:

Share one personal goal for the coming month.

Prompt:

What support do you need from me.

Presence Moment:

A brief, encouraging touch.

Day 24: Revisiting Shared Goals

Align your direction.

Practice:

Review one short term and one long term goal.

Prompt:

What is something we can build together this year.

Presence Moment:

Imagine the future together for ten quiet seconds.

Day 25: Vision for the Next Season

Discuss the coming months with intention.

Practice:

Each partner describes what they want the next season of life to feel like.

Prompt:

What emotional climate do you want to create at home.

Presence Moment:

Sit with the shared vision and breathe.

Day 26: Protecting the Relationship from Stress

Stress can disconnect couples if not discussed openly.

Practice:

Share your top stressors and one way your partner can support you.

Prompt:

What helps you feel held during stress.

Presence Moment:

A supportive gesture or touch.

Day 27: Creating a Connection Ritual

Rituals sustain connection.

Practice:

Design one small ritual to repeat weekly:

a walk

coffee together

evening check in

shared gratitude

Prompt:

What ritual feels natural and joyful.

Presence Moment:

Seal it with affection.

Day 28: A Love Letter Moment

Words matter.

Practice:

Write three sentences describing what you treasure about your partner.

Read them aloud.

Prompt:

What was meaningful about hearing that.

Presence Moment:

Hold each other gently.

Day 29: A Future Gratitude

Imagine the future and express gratitude in advance.

Practice:

Each partner completes:

One thing I will appreciate about us a year from now is...

Prompt:

What do you hope we continue to cultivate.

Presence Moment:

Smile at the idea of your future selves.

Day 30: Celebration and Renewal

Today you celebrate your journey.

Practice:

Share:

three things you learned

three moments that felt special

one commitment you want to carry forward

Prompt:

What does connection feel like for you today compared to Day 1.

Presence Moment:

Hold each other and let the journey settle into your hearts.

Closing Thoughts on the 30 Day Journey

This journey is not the end. It is the beginning of a deeper chapter in your relationship. These practices give you tools you can return to again and again. They keep your connection alive, responsive and resilient. The small daily conversations and acts of presence become emotional threads that strengthen your bond.

When couples practice connection with intention, love becomes steadier, safer and more fulfilling. The journey creates a rhythm of closeness that sustains you through change, stress and growth.

Your relationship is not fixed in time. It is a living, evolving space. You now have a structure to nurture that space with care.

www.ingramcontent.com/pod-product-compliance
Lightning Source LLC
Chambersburg PA
CBHW052015070526
44584CB00016B/1760